A Rainbow Book

D0870008

Slow

and

Steady

Hiking the Appalachian Trail

ROBERT A. CALLAWAY

Rainbow Books, Inc.
FLORIDA

Slow and Steady: Hiking the Appalachian Trail
© 2014 by Robert A. Callaway

Softcover ISBN 978-1-56825-157-8
EPUB e-book ISBN 978-1-56825-158-5

All photos are by the author or are used by permission of the photographer.

Published by

Rainbow Books, Inc.
P. O. Box 430
Highland City, FL 33846-0430

Editorial Offices and Wholesale/Distributor Orders

Telephone: (863) 648-4420
Facsimile: (863) 647-5951
RBIbooks@aol.com
RainbowBooksInc.com

Individuals' Orders

Toll-free Telephone (800) 431-1579
Amazon.com (Kindle edition available)
BN.com (Nook edition available)
AllBookStores.com (search by title, choose "compare prices")

The paper used in this publication meets the minimum requirements of the American National Standard for Information Sciences—Permanence of Paper for Printed Library Materials, ANSI Z39.48-1984.

First Edition 2014

18 17 16 15 14   6 5 4 3 2 1

Printed in the United States of America.

To Tommy Callaway, my brother, whose humor
and problem-solving ability were welcome on the trail,
and to Jane Callaway, my wife, who took over all duties
at home for nine months and made my hike possible.

Contents

Chapter 1

The Obsession

I learned of the Appalachian Trail when I was eight years old.

My mother was working at the kitchen sink, reminiscing about my granddad, her father. Granddad had wanted to hike the trail, she told me. But sadly he had died of cancer in 1949 (I was four years old then), a year after Earl Shafer finished his thru-hike of the Appalachian Trail. Shafer's hike was the first documented complete thru-hike, and it was publicized in all the newspapers. That is probably where Granddaddy got the idea of hiking the trail.

Over the next four decades I would, on occasions, think of Granddaddy's unfulfilled wish. I had a vague notion of one day hiking the trail to finish what he had planned. But I was never obsessed with the idea until I reached my forties.

It happened this way.

At age forty-six I joined the Adventure Cycling Association, a bicycle touring/advocacy organization that sponsors long distance cycling tours. The bike tours follow several east-west and north-south routes. The distances vary from several hundred miles to over 4,000 mile, cross-America expeditions.

In 1992, when I was forty-seven, I signed up for a 450-mile, ten-day tour in New England. Having only limited time off from the hospital where I worked as a physician, I chose that relatively short tour. We put in between fifty to sixty miles of biking each day with loaded panniers. We camped each night and took turns cooking for the group, which consisted of twelve bikers and one leader.

Over those ten days, life for a group member was simple: you pedaled for about six hours and you helped the group buy groceries. After supper was prepared, you ate, you pitched your tent, you slept soundly, you woke up the next day — and did the same thing again. I loved it.

At home I read Adventure Cycling Association's monthly magazine and salivated over stories of long distance bike touring, and it rekindled my interest in doing the Appalachian Trail. At some point I discovered the Appalachian Trail Conservancy (ATC), which exists to protect and maintain the Appalachian Trail (AT) over its entire 2,175-mile length from Georgia to Maine. I joined the ATC, and after reading just a few of their bimonthly publications, in which members recount their trail hiking experiences, I became obsessed about hiking the entire trail, just as Granddaddy had hoped to do. But that day would have to wait. For the next decade and a half I never had enough time off from the hospital to do it.

However, over the next twelve years I did complete four section hikes during four separate summers to get a feel for what hiking was like.

I was forty-nine when I did my first hike in the summer of 1994. I chose a seventy-mile section of the trail between Sams Gap in North Carolina, where US 23 crosses, and Roan Mountain, Tennessee, where the trail crosses at US 19E.

I chose that starting point because I had flown from our home in Virginia with my son to drop him off at a summer camp in North Carolina. At the airport I hired a rental car to drive him the rest of the way to his destination. That done, I returned the car and caught a taxi to the AT at nearby Sams Gap.

I had calculated what I needed in the way of food, clothing and shelter. I had purchased a six-pound, external-frame backpack and a three-pound tent. When all items were put in the pack it weighed forty-five pounds. At that point (without pack) I stepped on the scales: I weighed 140 pounds without my boots. With five-pound military hiking boots and the backpack, I weighed 190 pounds, heavier by fifty pounds than what I was accustomed to. But never mind, I thought.

When I exited the taxi I was ready to hike, or so I thought.

Right away, my troubles began. I had a hard time finding the trail; I blundered around on one side of the mountain, then on the other. Finally, after some twenty minutes of vexation, I came across a sign welcoming foot traffic but excluding motorized vehicles and horses.

I was on the AT at last!

I started hiking north. It seemed like a steep, long ascent to Low Gap. Actually, it was a 300-foot ascent over two and a third miles from Sams Gap to Low Gap. It was during the climb that the shoulder straps of my pack started digging deeply and painfully into my shoulders, and I had to stop time after time and take it off to give myself a break.

About a mile into the climb, I met a young, southbound hiker whose trail name was Gypsy Wind. He was hiking from Damascus, Virginia to Hot Springs, North Carolina. He tried to boost my spirits by asserting that the climb would soon end and the hiking would be easier.

I resumed my northward hike, encouraged by Gypsy Wind. It was hot, it was painful, it was slow going. As Bill Bryson said in his book, *A Walk in the Woods,* of his first day on the AT: "It was Hell!"

At two miles I reached Street Gap, where the trail leveled out and hiking became easier. Then I came to Low Gap, and I called it a day after only three miles. The taxi had dropped me off at 3:00 p.m., and it was now 6:00. I had hiked roughly one mile per hour.

I pitched the tent, cooked a freeze-dried supper and went to bed. It was clear to me that I was carrying too much weight, but I'd have to wait until Erwin, Tennessee before doing anything about it.

It took me three days to hike the twenty-four remaining miles to the Chestoa Bridge at the Nolichucky River, which is close to Erwin. I arrived at the bridge weak and dehydrated, but I pushed on for a three-mile road walk into Erwin. I must have looked wasted when I took a break under the shade of a tree by the road.

A local man stopped his truck. "Do you want a ride to town?"

Yes, I did. I put my pack in the back of the truck and got into the cab. He took me to a mom-and-pop motel downtown.

The woman at the motel desk did not know how to process my credit card. That was okay with me; I had cash. I just wanted off the trail and to have a bed to sleep in.

I called my wife first, then my mother, to tell them that I was exhausted — but now I was back in civilization and recovering. Both thought my voice was weak. Mom even offered to drive from Georgia to pick me up. I declined the offer, stayed on at the motel for a second day to regain my strength and lighten my load by sorting through my pack. I planned to mail home clothes, books and even food. My pack was nine pounds lighter; therefore, I surmised the next section to the town of Roan Mountain, Tennessee should be easier.

I did that forty-mile section in four days. My pack was lighter, I was in better hiking condition after the first section, and I do not remember much trouble going up Roan Mountain, with the highest shelter on the AT — over 6,000 feet. From the south, the ascent up to Roan Mountain is very steep. I remember well in 2008, when I walked this section from north to south, that the descent southward after Roan Mountain was awful (see page 55). But ascending up Roan Mountain from the south in 1994 must not have been too tough for me because I don't remember it. I had lightened my pack, I had improved my hiking condition, and I was fourteen years younger. I do remember the rain, however, because it caused me to stop at Overmountain Shelter to spend an afternoon and night on the crowded second floor with other hikers who also were trying to escape from cold, blowing rain.

The following day I walked to Roan Mountain, Tennessee. As arranged, my wife picked me up.

In August 1995 — at the end of my fiftieth year — I decided to try again.

This time, I kept the pack weight at thirty-five pounds. I had driven my son to his summer camp in North Carolina in my own car, delivered him to his camp, then left my car at the airport and hired a taxi to take me to Sams Gap. I hiked *south* for 110 miles to Newfound Gap in the Smoky Mountains National Park. The hiking was not as miserable as it had been the year before, when I was overloaded and hiking north from Sams Gap.

A hiker complained about Big Butt Mountain in the log book at one of the shelters. "Big Butt kicked mine," read the note. But the climb up that mountain did not seem especially difficult to me. It took me eight hiking days to get to Newfound Gap. After that, I felt I was ready to take on the trail and needed only the time off from work to do it. But real time off never came as long as I worked at the hospital.

In the summer of 2004, at age fifty-nine, I took another AT section hike. Since my last hike I had aged nine years; however, I was confident that I could hike like I did in 1995. I planned to go from Reeds Gap on the Blue Ridge Parkway to Cloverdale, Virginia — over 100 miles to the south.

I parked my car at Reeds Gap/VA 664 one hot day and started hiking south. With the heat and high humidity I became dehydrated on my way up to Hanging Rock. I used up all my water, and it was even hotter and more humid at Three Ridges and Chimney Rock. I should have carried more water and less other weight.

While descending to Harper's Creek Shelter, I became so weak that I took out my sleeping bag and empty water bottles, and left my backpack on the trail. I got down the hill to Harper's Creek as best I could, walking and stumbling along. I was in a mental fog, and despite hearing a barking dog, which should have alerted me to the occupied, nearby shelter, I missed the sign to Harper's Creek Shelter. I came to the creek and realized I had missed the side trail to the shelter.

I filled my water bottles, backtracked to the shelter and joined four other hikers and their dog. I drank water, several bottles of it. It took several hours and more water for my voice to strengthen, for my pulse to slow and for my mind to become clear.

The next morning I hiked back up the trail and retrieved my pack. Then and there I decided it was too heavy. I had not weighed it before the hike. The lesson about overpacking that I had supposedly learned in 1994 had not been learned well enough. Further, my boots were too heavy.

It was time to take a hard look at myself and seriously reassess my situation. I had almost died the night before from dehydration. Was I in over my head? Was I too old? I wondered. Despite my long-standing practice of running twenty miles a week, I realized that I was not in *hiking* condition. I had to make changes before continuing toward Cloverdale, Virginia.

I took the pack downhill to the shelter and left it while I hiked with a lighter load of food and water, retracing my steps back to my car. Even with a light load I ran out of water and had to refill at Maupin Field Shelter.

Once I reached my car, I drove into Waynesboro, Virginia to buy new, less heavy boots and to recover with a day of rest at a motel. That night I studied the AT maps, trying to decide where to attempt my next section. But first I had to retrieve my backpack.

Slow and Steady

Come morning I returned to the AT at Tye River, three and a half miles south of Harper's Creek Shelter. I hiked to the shelter and was able to hike out with my very overweight pack.

At another motel I removed all the items from my pack that I felt I could do without: extra sets of trousers, socks, shirts, a jar of peanut butter and a book. Then I studied the trail to Cloverdale and chose a trailhead only forty miles north of town at Parker's Gap Road. I hiked the section in four days. It was easier because of the lighter pack and lighter boots, and because the trail had an overall 2,000 foot descent to Cloverdale. I also drank as much water as I could.

At Cloverdale I stayed at the Howard Johnson motel. I had left a bicycle there several days earlier, and the next day I biked back to my car and left for home. I felt that I had failed, that I had miscalculated both my abilities and the pack weight I could carry.

The experience on that trail was sobering.

I had learned — again — that I must limit weight, even more so than when I was ten years younger. I learned that I could get dehydrated easily. And I learned to respect the conditioning that hiking demands.

I hiked again in summer 2005 at age sixty. I took seriously the lessons from 2004, especially the danger of dehydration. I made certain that I drank plenty of water and always obtained new water at streams and springs.

My daughter, a student at Virginia Tech, drove me to nearby Pearisburg, Virginia, where I planned to hike north. But when I left Pearisburg northward for the Rice Field Shelter, I once again experienced the effects of not being in hiking condition. I struggled in the four-mile ascent from New River to a campsite where a spring flows.

I met seasoned hikers resting there who had been on the trail from Springer Mountain, Georgia. They assured me that, with time, my legs would strengthen to the point that I would not notice the hills. They moved on, but I later joined them again at Rice Field Shelter.

I was beaten down after only six miles and could not continue. I did not hike on to the next shelter as I had planned. It was twelve miles away, and I had been knocked out by a mere six miles the day before. So I turned back to Pearisburg. It was easier hiking going down, and I was very happy to rest for the night in a motel room and lick my wounds. I wondered if I would *ever* be up for hiking the trail.

I got back on the trail the morning after at Pearisburg, but this time I hiked south. I ascended two miles to Angels Rest then six miles farther to Docs Knob Shelter. I was tired — but pleased — to make over eight miles. Along the way I met a conditioned northbound hiker who had come seventeen miles that day — from a campground on VA 606, where he had received good food and satisfactory camping accommodations.

So, encouraged by my progress, the following day I hiked over eight miles to Wapiti Shelter. I was hiking stronger, and water supplies were good along the route. I followed that feeling the next day and hiked nine more miles to the campground on VA 606, where I had a real hamburger meal and a shower. I then turned around and did a three-day return to Pearisburg. When I arrived I was hiking stronger than ever.

After a night in a motel, I hiked north again to Rice Field Shelter. The six-mile hike up to the shelter was much easier than the first time I had tried it, only a week earlier. I returned to Pearisburg the next day, and my daughter picked me up as planned and took me to the Greyhound Bus Station in Roanoke, Virginia, where I caught a bus home.

With this hike I had developed my hiking legs; by keeping my pack lighter, I avoided weight problems of the past year; by being careful to drink, I had avoided dehydration. The quick improvement

Chapter 2

The Beginnings

March 21, 2008 to April 15, 2008

I loved my work at the hospital, but the time had come.

Since I would need at least nine months to hike the Appalachian Trail, and I was sixty-three years old, it seemed like now or never. Though I had been an active runner for forty-five years, typically running twenty miles a week, my running time had increased with age. Twenty years earlier I ran four miles in under thirty minutes. Now the same four miles took me forty minutes.

In other words, as I looked back over the past, my hiking strength had declined when I compared my section hikes of 1994 and 1995 with those in 2004 and 2005. I did not want to miss my chance to hike the AT by waiting too long to do it; so, the decision was made: In 2008, I "retired."

Now about my already retired brother Tommy . . .

Tommy was in his late fifties, overweight, out of condition, and when I asked him to join me on the hike, "No way," was his reply.

I told him, "You can lose weight on the trail, get in better condition and learn to enjoy hiking."

To get Tommy in the right frame of mind, I even sent him Bill Bryson's book, *A Walk in the Woods*.

Tommy laughed and laughed as he read about Bryson's AT experiences. He admitted that it was great fun reading about someone else's miseries on the trail. Whether he could tolerate such miseries *himself*, he was not so confident. However, shortly after reading Bryson's book, he decided to give it a try and agreed to hike with me for as long as he could put up with it.

"If it gets too miserable," he said, "I'll go home."

I agreed. It was a common sense thing to do.

We worked out the timing and decided that we would set off in late March 2008. I sent Tommy some hiking gear, such as a GoLite backpack. I told him it was imperative to keep the pack weight at or below twenty-five pounds. I also sent him a Big Agnes tent and several items of clothing. To top that off, he went to an outfitter in Atlanta where he was fitted with boots and given a pep talk by a young salesman.

The salesman had hiked the AT the year before — in five months. "Hell, it's just walking," he told Tommy. Then he regaled Tommy with stories of hikers he'd met along the way who were as unconditioned as Tommy. All of them had done well, and he encouraged Tommy to give it a try.

Another worker at the outfitter pulled Tommy aside and asked him if he knew what he was getting into. "Man, I tell you, you don't stand a chance — unless you lose that beer gut."

Tommy pointed out that the man talking had a sizeable gut of his own.

When pressed, the man admitted that he liked his beer just as much as Tommy.

Tommy preferred the opinions of the young salesman and even wrote a letter to the outfitter management about how helpful he had been. Tommy was getting into the spirit of this adventure, it seemed.

I was pleased for him and began to look forward to the day when we would head out.

Every year hundreds of people attempt to hike the entire Appalachian Trail. They usually begin at the southern terminus, Springer Mountain, Georgia and then hike northward, hoping to reach the northern terminus at Katahdin, Maine.

The majority of hikers eventually terminate their hike for various reasons: some have injuries, some have to go home to take care of domestic problems, some run out of money. But the most common reason for quitting is loss of the original enthusiasm that brought them to the trail in the first place. The hills, the rain, the heat, sometimes the loneliness, and the unending daily grind of mile after mile can slowly sap one's will to continue. Tommy and I read the statistics: About ten percent of hikers who start out at Springer make it to Katahdin.

We went in with our eyes wide open.

Tommy told his friends about his plans, and some made bets about how long he would last. Most felt he would quit after a week. Only his daughter and I thought he might make it all the way. For my own part, I told as few people as possible about my plans. I did not want to explain myself to others, should I have to abandon the trail. We agreed to start in Georgia and proceed north.

I debated with myself about the next strategy. I had what I thought was a great idea: Why not use two vehicles? Park one south, like at

Springer Mountain, and park the other twenty miles north, like at Woody Gap? Leaving the northern vehicle, we would hike south to Springer. Then we would take the vehicle parked at Springer and drive north beyond Woody's Gap and park it at an AT road crossing. From there we would hike south to the vehicle parked at Woody's Gap. The idea was to proceed north, section by section, using a leap-frog, flip-flop method. That way, we could gradually grow accustomed to the rigors of hiking and increase the distance as we gained fitness.

Even better, when we reached one of the vehicles, we had a way to escape to civilization — motels, supplies or restaurants. Having such an easy way off the trail was a major psychological benefit. It did away with anxiety about how to get into towns and about which road crossing to use to get into town. Also — and here was a real plus — we could keep food supplies in each vehicle, along with boots and tents and backpacks, should we need replacements.

Finally, I called Tommy to share my great idea with him. I asked him if he had a junk car, some "piece of crap" that we could use for trail shuttling. I offered my own 1992 Buick Century for the cause, and Tommy was able to borrow a 1986 Isuzu Pup pickup truck from his son. He agreed that the two-vehicle strategy was appealing. We both agreed that after we got used to hiking we could discard the cars.

We were finally ready!

I drove from my home in Chesapeake, Virginia down to LaGrange, Georgia, where Tommy lived. The next day we departed LaGrange and drove to Tommy's mountain ridge cabin, close to Ellijay, Georgia and psyched ourselves up for the start of our hike.

On a cold and windy March 21, 2008, we drove both vehicles to US Forest Service Road (USFS) 42 where it crosses the AT one mile

The author in front of his brother Tommy's cabin near Ellijay, Georgia.

north of Springer Mountain, the AT's southern terminus. We left the Isuzu truck in the trailhead parking lot. Then I drove us both to Woody Gap where GA 60 crosses the trail about twenty miles north of Springer Mountain. The Buick was left in the trailhead parking lot there.

We shouldered our packs, grabbed our hiking poles and were ready to set off to the south when I found that Tommy had no gloves. I went back to the car and brought out an extra pair of winter gloves for Tommy. We were now off — for better or worse.

The wind was cold and biting, and Tommy was thankful for the gloves. The hiking was easy for about the first mile, but then we came to hills and slowed down. After five miles we reached Gooch Gap Shelter. I decided to stop for the night, even though plenty of daylight remained. I did not want to overtax Tommy or myself on the first day.

At the shelter we met Night Walker, a hiker in his mid-forties who had stopped for a rest. He planned to walk on late into the night, his usual practice, and hence his trail name. He told us, "When the moon is out you can see well enough to stay on the trail without a headlamp." He talked on and on, giving us and several other hikers a great deal of advice about hiking, cooking and equipment. His speech was fluent and uninhibited. After an hour or so of talking, he hiked on to the north.

That night Tommy had difficulty sleeping. We slept in our sleeping bags on the wooden floor of the shelter. Shelters have three sides and a roof, which close off the wind and rain The fourth side is open to the elements, but the floor is usually far enough back from the open side to be safe from rain. A young woman, whose trail name I won't mention, snored heavily from the other side of the shelter. In the morning Tommy was in a sour mood from lack of sleep.

We boiled water for coffee and oatmeal on Tommy's small, natural gas stove, which we set on a wooden table outside the shelter. After eating, we started south.

It was a hard day, especially for Tommy, who was winded on each uphill, and we stopped frequently for rest. He also developed blisters on his toes, which didn't do much to encourage him. We did, however, make it to Hawk Mountain Shelter after a tough hike of eight miles.

Tommy talked at the shelter with Gator from Florida, a strong hiker in his mid-thirties. He had a happy outlook on trail life; his happiness provided us needed encouragement. Still, Tommy pitched his tent fifty feet away to avoid snorers, while I slept in the shelter. After a good night's sleep, we both felt better as we set out the next day.

Along the way we met a number of vigorous hikers going north while carrying packs of forty pounds or more. We wondered how the strong hikers were able to carry forty-pound packs so easily and envied them for their youth and vigor.

Our greatest astonishment came when we met a middle-aged man who identified himself as the CEO of GoLite LLC, the maker of the GoLite packs we were using. He was resting on a log with a gigantic backpack strapped on. He saw our packs and was thrilled that we were using his product. Carefully maintaining his position on the log, he took our pictures and spoke into a cassette recorder identifying us and where he met us. He claimed that his massive pack had 125 pounds in it — mostly food — to sustain him on a forty-day field test of his expedition pack. When he stopped to rest with his pack on, he had to position himself so he could pull it back up. It must have been easier to rest with the pack on than to take it off then try to get it back on again. We wondered how he did it as we hiked onward.

After seven miles we reached the Springer Mountain trailhead and gladly put our packs into the back of the Isuzu. I wanted to do the last mile up to the top of Springer, but Tommy was exhausted and wanted to leave. He pulled out his cell and told his son that he was "give out." I did not insist on that last mile up to Springer; instead, we got in the truck and left. (That last mile stayed on my mind until I finally took care of it in December 2008.)

Tommy at
Springer Mountain trailhead.

Me at Springer Mountain trailhead. The trail not taken — for now.

On the way down USFS 42, a tire blew and we had to replace it. We drove back to Tommy's cabin to recuperate.

After a good night's sleep, we awoke to a "zero" day, a day during which you don't walk on the trail. We rested at Tommy's cabin, and Tommy cooked. His wife Sherry visited us and listened to our stories about snorers, hikers with heavy packs, our sore feet and how good it was to be back in civilization.

Tommy had found all the hikers friendly and safe to be around. He also discovered that most were of liberal mentality — more inclined to vote Democratic and to have open, accepting attitudes about alternative lifestyles. Tommy is a church-going Republican with conservative views about work, government and lifestyles. The hikers may have been misguided, from Tommy's viewpoint, but they were not personally threatening. He discarded the pistol he had carried, realizing that he did not really need it. Sherry took it back to LaGrange.

We were now ready for the next section.

Tommy in front of his cabin.

Tommy drove the Isuzu up to Tesnatee Gap/PA 348, and we hiked south until we reached the Walasi-Yi Outfitters and Hostel at Neels Gap at US 19. The hostel is literally on the trail, which passes under an arch that sits physically over the basement sleeping quarters. It had been a cold six miles in a light but blowing snow. We were glad to stop and paid for two bunks. For the rest of the day we just hung out, browsed through the outfitter store and bought hot dogs at the grill. The Walasi-Yi is a friendly hiker-oriented place. It helps hikers mail home contents of overweight packs and sells hiker supplies.

That night, Tommy and I ate soup and crackers fixed by Pirate, a bearded former hiker who cooks and oversees the living quarters. For the night, all twenty bunks were taken by cold, weary hikers, and one even spent the night on a couch in the common TV room.

Pirate explained, "We try to accommodate all comers and almost never turn away a hiker."

The sixty-eight degree temperature inside felt very good.

When we went to our bunks for the night, Tommy found the young woman snorer from Gooch Gap Shelter was to sleep on the bunk below him, so we switched bunks and we both slept well.

Tommy woke me at 6:00 a.m. I wanted to sleep on in the warm bunk, but he wanted to get going. We ate Pirate's bacon and eggs and took off.

Tommy was getting stronger. We went up Blood Mountain without excessive stopping. But he had blisters, which were painful on the downhill sections.

We again met the CEO of GoLite, seated on a log and talking seriously on his cell phone. From bits I could overhear, it sounded like the office wanted him back for some big decision. (Later we heard he was indeed called back to his company, and when he reached the Walasi-Yi, he mailed back the contents of his big pack and left the trail.)

We pushed on, and after eleven miles we reached Woody Gap/ GA 60 by 3:45 p.m. We were tired, and the Buick looked like a million dollars. I drove down to Suches, Georgia, where Tommy picked up a parcel from the post office just as it was closing at 4:00 p.m. His wife had sent him a pair of hiking shoes to replace his blister-producing, larger boots. We then drove back to Tommy's cabin after picking up Nathan's hot dogs at the Food Lion grocery store. It had been a good day, and the hot dogs and beer went well together.

I said, "I like this luxury hiking!"

And Tommy agreed.

The next morning we drove to Dicks Creek Gap close to Hiawassee, Georgia, where US 76 crosses the trail, and started what we planned to be a three-day, thirty-mile hike.

The first day we did eleven miles to Tray Mountain Shelter, where we found a friendly, rotund man, whom I will call Mr. X, and his son already in the shelter. He was a retired counselor. (I have tried not to use his name and other definitive info. He might read the book and take offense.)

Tommy had a hard day of climbing, and we were too tired to put up our tents. I suspected Mr. X would turn out to be a snorer, but I said nothing to Tommy and just hoped for the best. We soon went to bed and to sleep. Not long afterward we were startled awake by the most god-awful snoring I have ever heard. Mr. X was at it with a vengeance.

Several explosive snorts were followed by loud, regular snores, which were followed by prolonged pauses. After the forty-five-second period of quiet, the cycle was repeated. This continued all night, and sleeping for us was impossible. We should have tented out a long distance from the shelter, but it was so cold and we were so tired, we just suffered through the night.

Tommy fell asleep several times; I know because I heard *him* snore. The only relief we enjoyed was when Mr. X woke up at 4:00 a.m. for reading, but at 5:00 a.m. he went back to sleep and was back at it again.

Before we departed in the morning, I left a note about Mr. X's snoring in the shelter log with the hope that he would read it and realize how his snoring impacted others. "He should sleep in a tent well away from shelters," I wrote. (We heard later that he became employed at a hiker hostel, but he was required to sleep in a tree house, far from the regular sleeping quarters.)

We hiked out at 7:00 a.m. Soon Tommy began to have pain over the left knee in the lower thigh. It became much worse as we climbed Rocky Mountain. After six miles we reached GA 75 at Unicoi Gap, and Tommy had to stop.

I recommended that he pitch his tent, and I would cover the next fifteen miles to Tesnatee Gap and drive back to pick him up.

But Tommy, being the resourceful person he is, trusted his luck at thumbing a ride to town and then getting a taxi to Tesnatee Gap. He thumbed a ride, and some Good Samaritan stopped and took him the fifteen miles to Tesnatee Gap, where the Isuzu was parked, thus avoiding a trip to town and a taxi. The man refused Tommy's offer of payment. (Tommy later wrote a letter to the local newspaper editor about the Good Samaritan.)

From there Tommy drove back to get me at Unicoi Gap, and for the next two days we stayed at Tommy's home in LaGrange while he rested his sore leg.

There was good news, too.

Tommy's blisters had improved with the new hiking shoes, and his sore leg quickly improved with rest and analgesics. And, so far, I was doing well with neither blisters nor pain.

On the trail and off, Tommy was able to recount old stories of our lives at home as teenagers and schoolboys — when our parents were alive.

"Now, Bobby, wipe that frown off your face," Mom used to tell me, and Tommy was able to repeat it just like it was said, along with her expressions. "Take that frown and turn it upside down" or "Why, Bobby!"

If I seemed tired or in a funk, Tommy would bring those admonitions back from the past, while I chuckled in spite of myself.

And he quoted Dad, saying, "Not enough sugar for a dime," when I came back huffing and puffing after filling water bottles from a spring down a steep side trail.

Tommy had a special skill at solving problems — like thumbing that ride back to his truck. He was expert at putting up a tent and using a tarp he found on the trail. He can also fix anything wrong with a car. His special skills were a real asset on the trail.

After the restorative rest in LaGrange, we returned to the trail at Tesnatee Gap, once we'd juggled the vehicles. This time we hiked north toward Unicoi Gap, thereby avoiding the steep ascent out of Unicoi Gap. This gave Tommy's leg a better chance of avoiding re-injury. We hiked the next two days without any problem except for rain.

On the second day we met Joyce, a young woman in her mid-twenties who had been granted six months leave from her job in Maine. She worked in the state microbiology lab and was walking the trail back home. Her parents had dropped her off at Springer, and despite her mother's tears, she was hiking the trail alone. She passed us easily, but complained about a sore leg.

During a lunch break at Blue Mountain Shelter, we offered Joyce transportation from Unicoi Gap to a motel where she could rest her leg. At first she accepted, but then the rains stopped and the sky cleared — so beautiful that she decided to stay and recuperate at the shelter. She had plenty of food, so we wished her luck and hiked on to Unicoi Gap. We had done sixteen miles in two days. Tommy's leg was good — he was getting even stronger.

As we had finished the last section of hiking north — we did only two sections hiking north — we had to recover my Buick from Tesnatee Gap. During the drive, the Isuzu had another blowout. After changing the tire and recovering my Buick, we drove back to Ellijay and had three new tires put on the Isuzu to reduce chances of future blowouts. We then went to Dicks Creek Gap on US 76 and left the Isuzu. We drove the Buick back to Tommy's cabin and planned the next section.

When Tommy telephoned his wife Sherry to let her know we had returned once again to the cabin, she laughed at how tentative our hiking seemed to be!

At the cabin we mapped out our next section, thirty-five miles from Rock Gap, close to Standing Indian Campground in North Carolina, through to Dicks Creek Gap in Georgia. For two of the three days of that hike, it rained.

The rocky descent down Albert Mountain on the first day was treacherous. We found the modern shelter at Carter Gap full, but a

The Buick in front of Tommy's cabin near Ellijay, Georgia.

hiker told us about an old abandoned shelter less than a tenth of a mile away — and we slept in it by ourselves.

The next day Tommy felt exhausted on the numerous ascents, so we stopped at Standing Indian Shelter for the night, though we had done only eight miles.

A group of teenage girls was at the shelter, and I thought it must be full. But the girls were part of a Scout troop and were huddled in the shelter because their tents were too cold. Their presence crowded the shelter so much that is was nonfunctional. The leader realized it, and after passing the word, they left for their tents, and space became available to us.

We were glad to be in the shelter, the rains were heavy.

Soon after we settled in the shelter, two women in their sixties came in. The shelter was full after two more hikers arrived. Additional hikers came and had to tent out.

Tommy continued to struggle with ascents. He had to stop and rest frequently to catch his breath and restore his muscles. We went slowly, but we made it to the Georgia line, where with Tommy's cell phone we took pictures of the famous tree that grows there. Unfortunately, the photo was inadvertently deleted.

That night we stayed at the three-story Plum Orchard Gap Shelter in Georgia. There we met Baltimore Jack, who claimed he'd hiked the AT seven times. He had a supply of beer, whiskey and pizza. Tommy declined the offer of alcohol, and we cooked our own freeze-dried fare. Baltimore Jack talked and talked to Tommy and a number of other hikers.

Sleeping that night in the shelter was hard, especially for Tommy — more snorers.

Three young women from Maine were also there, and the snorers kept them awake too. They mimicked the two heaviest snorers with loud snorting noises, but it made no difference. Then one of the girls woke up a snorer and asked him to turn over. That helped for a short time, but the snoring soon started again in full force.

In the morning, Tommy was out of sorts; the snoring had kept him awake. But the sun was out and the rains had gone. We managed to get off and hiking again.

We made slow progress up the hills. While taking a rest, we met two young men in their early twenties who were hiking easily with large packs on their backs. We asked them how much they were carrying. With some reflection they remembered they were each carrying about fifty pounds.

One complained about pains in his foot, and Tommy gave sincere but doubtful advice about how to help his foot mend. I remained silent, knowing enough to know that I could not help him. (My medical expertise is in internal medicine and pulmonary medicine — not in orthopedics and podiatry.) Despite the foot pain, they soon set off, gliding easily up the next hill and out of sight.

We just shook our heads in disbelief.

When we reached Dicks Creek Gap and the waiting Isuzu, four young hikers had just arrived. We drove them seven miles to the Blueberry Patch Hostel in Hiawassee, Georgia, where space was available for them to rest. And, yes, we again returned to Tommy's cabin.

I had to reassure an amused Sherry, "Yes, we are serious about hiking the trail. We have already finished Georgia. We're ahead of schedule!"

Not really, and she knew it. We were behind schedule and going very slowly. "But at least we are still going, and, despite having to stop and rest frequently, Tommy is still into the hike," which was, hopefully, reassuring to her.

We began our next section at Tellico Gap/NC 1365 in North Carolina.

Leaving the Isuzu at 1:00 p.m., we hiked nine miles south to reach Wayah Shelter late in the day. Tommy did not want to risk being kept awake by snorers, and after filling our water bottles at a nearby stream we pushed on one-half mile farther to an empty campsite. There we pitched our tents, cooked supper and went to bed. Soon afterward, we heard groaning.

I grabbed a hiking pole and unzipped my tent, expecting to encounter a bear snooping around for food. Instead we found a young man doubled over on the ground, groaning and retching. He claimed he felt worse than he had ever felt before. He said he had eaten some wild onions that disagreed with him. He was so incapacitated with his pains and dry heaving that I knew we would have to help him.

We pitched his tent for him and got him inside with his sleeping bag so that he could at least lie down and rest with cover and warmth. He continued retching, and I talked to Tommy about calling 911 on Tommy's cell phone.

The young man overheard our talk and called from the tent that he wanted to get over it without calling in the rescue team. He had been having the GI upset for only a few hours. He was not yet seriously dehydrated, so I followed his wishes. I put his pack close to his tent door and gave him two bottles of our precious four-bottle water supply. He was to drink the water when the dry heaving stopped.

I listened for several hours and the retching and groaning seemed to slowly decrease. After midnight the retching noises from his tent ceased.

The morning after he was markedly improved. He identified himself as Bones. He had been able to drink both water bottles during the night, and his dry heaves were now gone.

We retrieved our empty bottles, took down our tents and wished him good luck. I told him about a water source that was down close to the shelter, and we hiked on.

By mid-afternoon we came to Winding Stair Gap, where US 64 crosses the AT. Tommy wanted to thumb a ride into Franklin, North Carolina to pick up a parcel sent to us from my wife. He did catch a ride and was able to pick up the parcel at the post office before it closed at 4:00 p.m.

In the meantime, I hiked for another four miles to my car at Rock Gap. I drove into Franklin, picked up Tommy at the post office and drove from there back to Tommy's cabin (one more time) in Georgia. The next day we had a zero day at the cabin while I worked on tax forms from the IRS that my wife Jane had sent in the parcel.

Now we were ready for another section.

We said goodbye to the Buick in the Fontana Dam Visitor Center parking lot and began a four-day, forty-mile hike. After a tough five-mile climb, we were resting at a campsite when Bones and a friend came along the trail. Bones recognized us and came over to shake my hand.

Bones had completely recovered from his gastrointestinal upset of three days earlier. He and his friend were going north at about twenty miles a day. When they moved onward I was convinced we would never see him again; they were moving ahead swiftly. Soon after that, we also saw the two young men we had met on our last day in Georgia — the ones carrying fifty-pound packs.

Tommy complained about the five-mile climb out of Fontana and about how slowly he was going. The tallest of the two turned around, and, pointing to Tommy, said, "Slow," then he pointed toward me and said, "Steady." Thus we took on the trail names, Slow and Steady, which we kept for the duration and which title this book.

Some say it is better to use the names given to you by fellow hikers than to use your own trail name. In Georgia we had tried out The Backtrackers, but it never seemed to catch on, whereas Slow and Steady seemed to be an immediate hit with us and with others.

Again we watched them with envy as they glided away easily with their large packs. The hiker with the sore foot had apparently gotten over it.

Soon after that we met another northbound hiker, Gator, who we had encountered several times. He was looking forward to meeting his girlfriend (or wife) who was waiting for him at Fontana. Despite having trouble from a long, steep ascent from the Nantahala River the day before, he had a decided spring in his step.

We hiked to Cable Gap Shelter. Rain had been forecast, and I persuaded Tommy to stop there for the night, though we had gone only seven miles. We met Cheeseburger and Aaron, both young men in their mid-twenties. I was glad we stopped; the rains did come in heavy for the night.

Neither Tommy nor I could sleep because of snoring in the shelter. We were dry the next morning, but the snoring had kept us both from getting much needed rest.

We hiked on to Brown Fork Gap Shelter where we cooked ramen noodles for lunch and refilled water bottles. That afternoon several hikers told us of upcoming "Trail Magic." Soon we met the three young women from Maine, who we had last seen them at Plum Orchard Gap Shelter in Georgia. They also spoke of Trail Magic ahead.

When we reached Stecoah Gap where NC 143 crosses the trail, we were invited to eat hot dogs, hamburgers and soft drinks under a large tarp setup. The person responsible for these wonders was Hopeful, a sixty-one-year-old former thru-hiker. He had hiked the trail several years earlier and used that trail name. Some south-bounder, close to completing the trail, had told him at Stecoah Gap always to be hopeful. He kept that name for his entire northbound hike, and every year on his birthday he dispensed Trail Magic to all AT hikers at Stecoah Gap. This birthday, we were a pair of lucky recipients.

Hopeful was being helped by Circuit Rider, also a former thruhiker, who had a ministry directed to the needs of hikers. About ten other hikers were enjoying the Trail Magic when we arrived.

Trail Magic is the kindness of others offered to hikers along the trail. It often comes as food. Sometimes it is an offer of a ride into town or to the grocery store. It always means "going out of one's way" to help hikers. After an hour of food and resting, we hiked on and told several northbound hikers we met about the Trail Magic awaiting them.

Later, one of the northbound hikers told me that, thanks to my information, he had hurried along and did get treated to hot dogs, hamburgers and soft drinks — just before they closed everything down for the day. The goodies had cheered him on, and he just wanted me to know.

That night we tented at Locust Cove Gap. Tommy called out to me once to stop snoring. I turned over, and he claimed he didn't hear any more out of me that night.

The following day we stopped at Sassafras Gap Shelter to use the privy. One advantage of most shelters is that there is a privy, which saves you the trouble of having to go in the woods. Not all are enclosed with four sides; some, in fact, have no sides and you have to do your business on a "throne" in the woods, completely exposed. If there is no one else around, it's no problem; but, if the shelter is occupied, you can only hope for privacy, which, sometimes you have and sometimes you don't have. But the privy at Sassafras Gap Shelter had four walls and excellent privacy, though I encountered graffiti galore, such as:

JESUS SAVES

MOSES INVESTS

I WISH JESUS WOULD SAVE MY SORE ASS

I WISH JESUS WOULD SAVE THIS TOILET

We next did the long, steep descent to the Nantahala River and the Nantahala Outdoor Center where US Highways 19 and 74 cross the trail. We took a room at the center and that night had a real meal with too much beer — but we felt we had earned it!

The day after, we made the steep ascent out of the Center in blowing snow. We encountered an older hiker, probably in his mid-seventies. He appeared not up to the task of hiking; he wore tennis shoes instead of hiking boots and had socks on his hands for mittens. He seemed tired and drenched from the snow. He was accompanied by a younger hiker who was in better condition.

"The Nantahala Outdoor Center is at the end of this long descent," I told them. "Just stay on the trail."

Tommy inquired, always his genial self, "Can we help? Do you need anything?"

The young man said, "Thanks, but we're okay."

We watched them go on along, and I was glad that the old man had a strong, attentive companion.

Later we met two young men jogging along in the snow, identical twins from Michigan. Time Cop and Danger Snake were their trail names. These young bucks had already done twenty miles that day, and it was only mid-afternoon when we met just south of Wesser Bald Shelter.

We reached Tellico Gap, glad to see the Isuzu waiting, and we drove back to the Fontana Dam Visitor's Center, exchanged the truck for the Buick, and returned to Tommy's cabin.

We took a zero day on April 15th. Tommy had to stop and finish his taxes.

At that point, we had been hiking almost a month. Truth is, we had hiked nineteen of the past twenty-five days and had improved our hiking condition. Tommy had lost twenty-five pounds and was stronger. In fact, Tommy had improved to the point that, on level sections and on downhills, he was faster than I was. I tended to walk in the lead, but Tommy began to tell me to speed up and to stop daydreaming, as it seemed to him that I was letting my mind get lost on the easy sections. However, on the uphills I was faster, having less weight to carry. I weighed 140 pounds; Tommy was 245 pounds. Both of our packs were the same — twenty-five pounds, excluding the weight of full water bottles, which I insisted we both carry — two each.

The rains had lessened my fears about dehydration, but I sometimes went off the trail to refill my water bottles. Tommy did not worry about dehydration and figured I was worried for no good reason. He thought it was funny as all get out that, after I expended great effort going a quarter mile off trail (down some long hill and back up again), we shortly came across a bubbling stream brimming with fresh rain water right on the trail. My motto: Better safe than sorry. I had experienced dehydration and Tommy had not.

I used AT guidebooks as a source of information when it came to water. The books don't tell you about rain-produced sources, but some do give advice about sources that are likely to be going dry. So, I did a number of needless searches for water, and Tommy started calling me Water Boy as a joke. But I still answered to the name Steady.

Meanwhile, Tommy remained involved in affairs with his family back in LaGrange. He missed being with them and called home several times a day to talk to Sherry and his two grown children. He would've been lost without his cell phone. I am devoted to family also, but I did not have any wish to call my wife or children *every* day. Different styles for different folks, I guess.

Tommy had otherwise accepted life on the trail. But when we got into the Great Smoky Mountains National Park, things would change . . .

Drying clothes at Tommy's cabin.

Chapter 3

Problems on the Trail

April 16, 2008 to May 8, 2008

After Tommy finished his taxes and had them postmarked on April 15, we drove the next morning to Newfound Gap, where US 441 crosses the AT, left the Buick in the parking lot and started south.

The day was mild and clear, but residual snow was a foot deep in some of the shaded spots. At first, we made good progress. Still, after several hours, Tommy wanted to get off the trail and "yellow blaze" to Clingmans Dome.

Yellow blazing is road walking to a destination. It is sometimes shorter in mileage, sometimes longer, but always easier than the trail. I resisted the idea and received support from the three girls from Maine who we met again while discussing road walking. The girls were the same northbound hikers we had met several times starting at Plum Orchard Gap Shelter in Georgia and throughout North Carolina. We kept meeting them as they moved north, section after section. We always hiked each section from north to south, while they kept hiking from south to north.

As a result, our meetings were frequent, always the "Hi-Bye" variety, except for the night we spent together at Plum Orchard Gap Shelter.

They asserted that the trail in front of us for the next few miles was not too bad. We journeyed onward. After eight miles we reached Clingmans Dome. We were tired, and Tommy was especially disgruntled at not taking advantage of easier road walking.

I am more of a purist about hiking. "Stay *on* the trail and do *all* the miles." That's my motto.

We stopped to rest near a short, side trail to the Park Service Lookout on top of Clingmans Dome, where one can get a panoramic view from the AT's highest point at 6,643 feet. But we were too tired to have any interest in taking that side trail. Four exhausted northbound thru-hikers came by, and they didn't take the side trail either. All of us had been in high peaks enough that day, and more were in front of us in both directions. Tommy and I kept going and finally reached Double Spring Gap Shelter, eleven miles from our starting point.

Though the park prefers to have hikers sleep in the shelters to avoid trampling the flora and compacting the soil outside of shelters, we made camp outside the shelter to avoid anyone who snored. As we were preparing supper, Tommy lost his balance from his perch on a log and fell over backward in a comical way. He let out a few choice curse words, while I kept my chuckles to myself. He was in no mood to share in any such merriment.

We slept well, and the morning after we did an easier seven miles to Derrick Knob Shelter. While taking a break there, we were warned by a hiker that the next section would be tough. We planned to push on to Spence Field Shelter. The going was indeed hard, especially the rocky heights around Thunderhead Mountain, which offered a beautiful 360-degree view. However, we were so tired that we had little energy to really enjoy it.

Further, I must admit I became impatient with Tommy. He had enough energy to call one family member after another on his cell phone, and the calls seemed overly long to me. I wanted to make the Spencer Field Shelter by sunset. We reached the side trail to what we thought was the shelter, only to encounter a sign that said the shelter was two-tenths of a mile farther.

We both let forth volleys of choice epithets and curses. We had more to say when we hiked on and came to another sign telling us the same thing. We didn't make it to the shelter until 7:00 p.m. It had been a thirteen-mile day with twelve hours of hiking.

To avoid snorers we pitched our tents in a paddock, a fenced-off flat place below the shelter, reserved for tethering horses. Evidently the site for horses had not been used for a long time; no horse droppings or even hoof prints were in sight. Again, we slept well.

On the following morning we were hoping to go all the way to Fontana, but I had my doubts about hiking fifteen miles. We met an AT Ridgerunner shortly thereafter who said, "I need to see your backcountry permit."

When I showed him the permit, he said, "Since you're only section hikers and not thru-hikers, you need a special number on the permit."

"We are thru-hikers," I responded vigorously. "We're using two vehicles and have been doing so since Springer." With that said, I quickly explained our process.

"Your complaints about being 'done in' by the trail are more typical of section hikers."

I repeated my assertion that we were legitimate thru-hikers.

He let it slide and added, "Don't forget. You should try to sleep in shelters unless they're full."

For the past two nights we had tented out at shelters, but neither of us responded to his admonition, remembering that hikers are subject to more rules and restriction in the Smoky Mountains National Park than in other sections. Such restrictions were used to protect the park and the trail, due to its heavy use. We issued a courteous goodbye and moved on.

When we reached Ekaneetlee Gap, I was worried about water and went off-trail and down to a spring — despite Tommy's protests that it would take too long. It was good that I refilled our water; we drank it all during the rest of the day.

Farther along the trail, we met other hikers looking for water, and I explained to them how to reach the spring.

After nine miles we arrived at Birch Spring Gap campsite, where I insisted we call it a day. I was tired and did not want to go six more miles to Fontana that day. Tommy was so tired he didn't argue, though he wanted to hike on.

We put up our tents on another flat spot where horses used to be tethered. We had easy access to a stream and refilled our water bottles. After we finished a freeze-dried supper, the rains came down heavily. Nevertheless, we slept snugly.

In the morning we took down our tents in the still-pouring rain. Our clothes and packs got wet, adding weight as well as discontent. We had six miles, mostly downhill, to Fontana.

Tommy began talking about dropping off the trail. The hiking had been hard, and he didn't think there was enough variety to make it any more interesting. He also missed his family.

I listened and let it go.

To add to our concerns, we'd heard about a closure of the Fontana Dam to hikers and asked several northbound hikers about a detour that would add two miles to the hike. Some hikers had done the two-mile detour and thought it was stupid.

One hiker could not suppress a smile when Tommy asked about the detour. He had crossed the Fontana Dam that morning — risking a fine — but no fine or citation had been issued. That was enough for Tommy. He was going for it; he was going to cross that dam and avoid the two-mile detour.

There was a safety concern about some cables on the dam; one had broken and there was the thought that others might also break. So, as a precaution, the operators of the dam were asking hikers to take a detour around it.

We arrived at the dam and found no clear cut directions to stay off it. Tommy took off across the dam, and I followed about thirty yards behind him. I was worried about being caught and had made up an excuse to use, if needed: The signs were unclear and confusing.

We arrived on the other side without trouble: no fine and no warning. Maybe Saturday morning was lucky for us; no workers were in sight.

The Isuzu pick up awaited, and we drove away in a happy frame of mind.

A big traffic jam caused us to divert away from our destination of Gatlinburg, Tennessee and a return to Tommy's cabin in Georgia. We

Back at the Tommy's cabin again, drying out sleeping bags and clothing on the balcony.

had a zero day there, during which Tommy's mood improved, and he decided to continue hiking. I had also needed a break and enjoyed the zero.

From Tommy's cabin we drove the Isuzu to Davenport Gap on the northest side of the Great Smoky Mountains Park, and for the next three days we hiked the thirty-three miles back to the Buick at Newfound Gap. Along the way we tented at both Cosby Knob and Pecks Corner Shelters.

On the second day we sat down for a lunch break just beyond Tricorner Knob Shelter. Two women also stopped there, and Tommy started talking to them. One hiker looked older (late sixties) than the other, and Tommy asked if the other hiker was her daughter.

Wrong question!

They were sisters, only nine months apart in age.

Shortly afterward, we sat down on a log close by the two women. I was eating and was paying no attention.

Tommy said, "Stop eating." I looked at him, and he motioned toward one of the women, who was retching.

I set aside my lunch and said, "Can I help you to the shelter?"

"No," she said.

But soon I found myself carrying her pack up the hill to the shelter. Her pack was heavier than mine and the climb up the hill was much longer than I had expected. I reached the side trail to the shelter, set her pack down for her to take to the shelter and wished her good luck. I then hurried off to join Tommy.

At the bottom of the hill I looked back up the trail. The woman was still looking at the pack as if undecided about whether to pick it up.

Tommy, quite diverted and jocular, asked me about whether I felt guilty for not going back to do it. I laughed at it too.

And the next day, when my back started hurting, Tommy ribbed me about showing off as a Good Samaritan and injuring my back in the process. And he laughed all the more when he began to wonder if he had not set off her retching by asking about her "daughter."

The two women were developing their hiking legs and were going through a rough patch. I was to see them several times more up north.

That night, after descending a three-tenths of a mile side trail to Pecks Corner Shelter, we tented out. We camped on a ridge next to the privy. Since the shelter was full, we were joined by two other campers. Exhaustion made everyone sleep well.

Before we departed in the morning, I refilled our water supplies below the shelter.

Tommy had recovered his typical jocularity. We encountered numerous horse droppings that day, and Tommy blamed it on the rangers patrolling the trail, though we didn't encounter any rangers. Horses are allowed on some trails in the Smokies, but sometimes riders went where they were prohibited.

We came to a side trail to Charlies Bunion, a lookout site over a large rock.

"F--- Charlies Bunion," Tommy muttered.

I nodded in agreement; I had little energy for side trips.

When we reached the Buick at Newfound Gap we drove to Gatlinburg, Tennessee and checked into the Bales Motel for a zero day. We had heard about this motel from a hiker, whose trail name was Hollywood, as we were approaching Clingmans Dome a week earlier. We had first met Hollywood in Georgia. We exchanged greetings, and he told us about how he and several other hikers had been well taken care of at the Bales when they had to leave the snowy trail at Clingmans Dome.

Tommy discovered he had a soul mate in the owner of the motel.

The man didn't believe in "left wing" ideas like taxes, welfare, environmental regulation or alternative lifestyles. I was surprised that he supported hikers, whose vagabond ways are a counterculture unto themselves.

We hung out there for two days, and I was able to do yoga exercises that Tommy thought crazy. In fact, the yoga exercises may have contributed to a flare up of back pains, a chronic recurring problem of mine. And I had noticed back pains the last day on the hike down to Newfound Gap.

It is surprising what luxury can do for two tired hikers. By luxury, I mean a real bed and real food and freedom from the need to carry a twenty-five-pound pack for twelve hours each day. Luxury is also having a warm shower with real soap and shampoo, followed by a feeling of cleanliness.

I did not need room service, which to me was carrying luxury too far, and told the lady who came to clean the room, "Don't bother. We'll only be here for a short stay. Then you can clean it. But thanks."

She nodded and went away, happy to be relieved of the chore.

Tommy felt I was cheating us out of what we had paid for.

I had read Barbara Ehrenreich's book, *Nickel and Dimed: On (Not) Getting By in America*, which details her undercover work in a number of low-wage jobs, including work as a room cleaner for a motel. Cleaners are badly overworked and badly underpaid, so I was motivated to give the room cleaner a break from cleaning our room. We really did not need room cleaning; our living conditions were vastly more luxurious than the trail.

When we departed the motel after a two-day rest, I left a tip for the room cleaner, and Tommy thought that was nuts. But one thing we both agreed on is that the motel was a welcome respite from the harsh conditions the trail presented.

We returned to the trail at Max Patch in North Carolina. Because of predicted rains and my back pain, I wanted a shorter hike of sixteen miles for the next two days.

We left Max Patch and came to Brown Gap, where a former thru-hiker had set up a tarp and offered Trail Magic: burgers, drinks and hot dogs. There we found Joyce S., a day hiker probably in her seventies. Her husband had dropped her off at Snowbird Mountain, and she had hiked north to Brown Gap — but she should have hiked south to Davenport Gap. She was trying to get a message to her husband, but there was no signal on her cell phone.

The Trail Magician had recommended that she stay there at Brown Gap, and, in the meantime, efforts would be made to contact her husband. Tommy tried his cell but no signal; it must have been the location.

Joyce did not know her husband's cell, but she did know his work number as well as her daughter's phone numbers. Tommy wrote down the numbers, and we proceeded south. Later he got a signal and contacted the husband's work and daughter's home numbers. He left messages with office workers and on the daughter's answering machine about Joyce's predicament.

Next we met Scout and Harvest. We had already met them twice. The young women had graduated from Virginia Tech in 2004 and 2003. Earlier we had met some hikers who asked us to help them perpetrate a trick on Harvest and Scout by telling them there was no Trail Magic at Brown Gap. Scout and Harvest wanted to know if the rumor was right or wrong.

"It's true," I said. "Yes, there is Trail Magic!"

They were pleased about the good news.

Then I added, "Your friends had told us to deceive you about the Trail Magic, but now you know the truth."

We met Harvest and Scout many times on the AT.

They were even more pleased at the failure of their friends to fool them.

We reached a campsite close to Snowbird Mountain and ended up pitching our tents in the rain. There we met Rainbow, a young woman in her late twenties, and her two dogs; they camped close to us. One of the dogs, a friendly, overgrown puppy, wiggled right into my tent, wagging its tail. (I was to meet Rainbow and her dogs several more times in Virginia.)

Later that night Tommy received a message on his cell phone that Joyce had been picked up by her family at Brown Gap.

We slept well, but my back was beginning to really hurt, and I had to position myself repeatedly during the night to get comfortable.

The following day we met Joyce's husband. He had again driven her up to Snowbird Mountain — this time she did hike south — and soon she came down the trail and met her husband, who was hiking north to meet her. He was very appreciative of Tommy's efforts of the day before.

My back was worse, much worse, and the downhills were difficult. I did better on the uphills.

But Tommy wasn't doing well. Once he just flopped down in the middle of the trail to rest and curse hiking!

We reached Davenport Gap and received more Trail Magic. Hot dogs and burgers were being served by a church group. There we again met Joyce and her husband and said goodbye.

We drove the Isuzu to Max Patch to get the Buick. Scout and Harvest were there, waiting for their boyfriends to pick them up. We gave them water because they had none. They then told us about spending the night and most of that day at Brown Gap, soaking up Trail Magic.

That night, close to Max Patch, we tried to sleep in the Buick, which was impossible. At midnight we gave up on the Buick, pitched our tents and spent the night on the ground. My back was really troubling me. I finally gave in to myself and said to Tommy, "I have to take time off the trail to rest my back."

Instead of returning to the cabin we drove to Tommy's home in LaGrange, Georgia. On the way down to LaGrange, Tommy asked me if I had ever been evaluated by a psychologist; that I obviously enjoyed hiking the trail seemed abnormal to him. Also he was concerned that I was not outgoing. Tommy is an extrovert and easily strikes up conversations with other people, whereas I tend to be more reserved.

I told him, "I did go to psychologists because of a family member's problems; I also went to Alanon. And I have never been called before a clinical competence committee at the hospital because of a suspicion of mental illness. And it is true, I am introverted, I guess, but I have always been like that — and you know it."

We had been out on the trail for over a month. Tommy usually stopped to talk to other hikers, especially if we had met them earlier. The connections he made with others often led to being helpful — like to Joyce, and to Harvest and Scout. We benefited too, such as the information about the Bales Motel. That came only from Tommy's interactions with his pal Hollywood.

But I did not pal around with others. I would help any hiker, if asked, and was free with advice about where the water sources were, and if I saw a hiker on the road I was sure to stop and offer a lift. But I did not readily establish friendships. So, Tommy had a point, and he was concerned about my being on the trail by myself, if he were not there to help me.

After four days at Tommy's house in LaGrange, my back was markedly improved, and we returned to the trail, taking the next segment north from Max Patch to Hot Springs, North Carolina. We had to shuffle the cars around, leaving one at Hot Springs and the other at Max Patch.

The first night we stopped at the Walnut Mountain Shelter. We were the only ones there, and Tommy agreed to sleep in the shelter instead of tenting. We were later joined by two other hikers, and, to Tommy's relief, they did not snore. There was, though, an incident in the night, so to speak.

I heard a racket and nudged Tommy awake. Immediately Tommy got up, turned on his headlamp, and spotted a big black bear feasting on our food, which we'd hung high in a tree outside.

"You sonavabitch!" Tommy yelled as he picked up a big rock and threw it, hitting the bear on the rump. The bear ran away, and Tommy put some of our food in a different place, but the next morning it too was gone. Likewise, the other hikers lost their food, even though they had hung theirs higher up than we had. So, the next morning, we all hiked, on empty bellies, the twelve miles to Hot Springs.

Trail Magic in the form of a cooler full of sports drinks, granola bars and crackers helped save the day at the halfway point, Garenflo Gap.

When we made it to Hot Springs we had supper at a diner, drove the Isuzu back to Max Patch and tented out at the parking lot.

Come morning we drove both vehicles back to Hot Springs and left the Buick in the public lot, then we drove the Isuzu to Sams Gap in North Carolina where I-26 and US 23 cross the trail. From Sams Gap we started the section that would prove to be Tommy's last three days on the trail.

Our first day was very easy: we went only as far as Hogback Ridge Shelter, less than three miles. Heavy rains had been predicted, and we decided to stop there to avoid getting drenched. As it turned out, no rain came, and, as Tommy pointed out, we lost a day's hiking as a result.

Anticipating a long hike on the next day, we started off early. We did nine miles relatively well and stopped at Flint Mountain Shelter for a lunch break. At the shelter we met Hike On, a retired USAF survivalist who had gone into trucking. He and Tommy exchanged views about trucking, something Tommy has wanted to do. Hike On had given up the trucking business to hike the trail.

He soon departed, and we started a long ascent toward Big Butt Mountain. It was tough going with long ups followed by longer ups to bends leading to who knows where. Tommy began an afternoon of cursing with numerous expressions that concerned fornication with ducks. I did much better on ascents and was not as exhausted.

In an effort to be more outgoing, I met and talked to a hiker our age, a retired doctor from Georgia, and asked him to try to boost Tommy's spirit by giving him a pep talk. But when he met Tommy, he told Tommy, "I am sick of the trail, I have foot pains and I am getting off at Sams Gap."

We finally arrived to the top at Big Butt and the trail became easier. When we reached Jerry Cabin Shelter we had done fifteen miles in twelve hours. We tented out and slept soundly.

We set out the next morning with a goal of doing fifteen miles to Spring Mountain Shelter, but the hiking was hard for Tommy. He vocalized discontent all morning. We stopped for lunch and water refills at Little Laurel Shelter then had a long downhill hike of four miles.

At Allen Gap Tommy decided to get off the trail and thumb a ride back to Hot Springs via NC 208. He said, "I've had enough," and that was it.

I watched him get into a passing van that stopped for him. He later reported that he was picked up by an eye doctor with wife and kids. He talked them into going out of the way to drop him at Hot Springs. Thinking that he would be refused, he offered a ten dollar bill to the doctor for his troubles, and the doctor "snapped it up like it was going out of style," according to Tommy's account. The wife was embarrassed and said it was not that much out of their way.

Tommy had other amusing off-trail tales to tell me later. He, of course, was glad to be back in Hot Springs and took a bunk at a hostel that night and slept without any snorers around. The following morning he checked into a motel room on the river and drove back to Sams Gap to check on the Isuzu. He noticed two hikers in the lot, thumbing a ride to Erwin, Tennessee. One was the doctor we had met two days earlier going up Big Butt. He hated hiking and was making good on his plan to quit the trail at Sams Gap. The other hiker, also a doctor, a psychiatrist, loved the trail and was going to Erwin for a motel room. Tommy took both to the Super Eight Motel in Erwin.

Tommy noted the psychiatrist had a habit of consulting a peach pit for decision-making. He suspended it on a string, let it swing back and forth and was able to divine some message from the swinging. He had used the peach pit to help decide to go down to Erwin for a night. He told Tommy that he also used this method professionally in the ER to help him decide which patient needed to be admitted. Tommy said he swore that this method was as good as any published methods in the psychiatric journals.

Tommy was a great storyteller, and he enjoyed reporting on that and other adventures.

Meanwhile, I had reached Spring Mountain Shelter. It was probably best that Tommy missed the three successive peaks from Allen Gap to the shelter; the climbs were really tough. The shelter was full, so I tented out, ate supper and refilled my water bottles from a source that was steeply downhill from the shelter. The next day I arrived at Hot Springs, where Tommy was waiting for me in the Buick.

Being something of a purist hiker, not wanting to skip any sections, I didn't want to be driven across the river. I hiked across the bridge to the other side of the river where I told Tommy to pick me up.

He thought I had gone off my rocker. He then drove me to the nice riverside motel, and I enjoyed a hot shower — heaven, indeed.

That evening at a local pub Tommy told me he would let me keep the Isuzu to help me continue on my northward trek. I would be able to flip the vehicles on my own. He also tried to set me up with a young northbound hiker who sat next to us in the pub. Tommy was not sure I could do the trail on my own without someone's help. But I did not want to connect with this fast-hiking young man. He had started out one month after we did, and he was already in Hot Springs. I would only slow him down, and I was confident that I would do well on my own.

The next day we drove up to Sams Gap for me to practice on the Isuzu, but I already knew how to drive a stick shift, and the lesson was quickly over. We met the peach pit psychiatrist who had just returned to the trail after luxuriating at the motel in Erwin. He thanked Tommy for his help the day before, saying a night in the motel was just what he needed.

The next day I drove Tommy to a town in north Georgia, halfway home, where his daughter Allison met us and drove him back to his house in LaGrange. He had given it his best for six weeks, had walked 310 miles, had lost thirty pounds and had become a much stronger hiker. But he never got to where he loved hiking, and he especially hated the uphills.

On his final day, he confided, "It is like getting an ass whipping every day — when you don't deserve it." The worst problem, over all others, was being away from his family. He just could not do without them.

I would hike on, but I would miss Tommy.

Later, Tommy would return to help me flip-flop up to Maine and start hiking south from there, but his own hiking days were finished. He considered himself free, like a runaway slave who had escaped from the old plantation: "Free at last, free at last!"

Chapter 4

On My Own

I would now have only myself to tend to . . .

I loved hiking, and I had confidence that I could quicken my pace. Tommy and I had been out for six weeks and had made 315 miles. At that rate, one would do the 2,175 mile trail in about ten months. Most of the hikers we met were faster, going at paces that would have them finish in five to seven months.

Tommy and I would meet a hiker repeatedly for two weeks, but sooner or later the hiker moved on northward and beyond where we had parked the advance vehicle. Bones, the young man who'd had the wild onion GI upset, was so fast we met him only twice, and then over only a four day period. Hike On we met only once. Later I saw both their entries in shelter logs and trail registers throughout Virginia. When I reached Harper's Ferry, Bones was a full month ahead of me.

Scout and Harvest were different. The young women were faster than we were, but they repeatedly took zero days off the trail to see boyfriends and family. As a consequence, we had met them about five times in North Carolina and the Smokies. They were about the same age as my daughter, who, like Scout, had graduated from Virginia Tech in 2004. I felt an almost paternal interest in their well-being. Their ready friendliness was always welcome and psychologically uplifting.

So, when I dropped Tommy off, I returned to the trail — hoping I would go fast enough to keep up with some of my hiker friends. I parked the Buick at Iron Mountain Gap, where TN 107/NC 226 cross the trail, and started a forty-three-mile section back to the Isuzu parked at Sams Gap.

After a few miles it was threatening rain; I decided to try for a dry spot in Cherry Gap Shelter. Upon arrival I found the place filled, and more hikers were to come in later. I quickly pitched my tent between two spruce trees — good protection from the now falling rain. Though I slept well, in the morning I had to take down my tent in the rain under dripping spruces. Before departure, I watched a hiker collect drinking water from run off that overflowed the shelter's rain gutters.

Fortunately, before setting out for the day's hike, I had wrapped my backpack in the blue tarp that Tommy had picked up at a shelter in North Carolina. It was warm enough that I eventually had to strip down to a cycling jersey and tie my rain gear onto my pack.

In the afternoon I again met Scout and Harvest after I had hiked past Beauty Spot — not so beautiful in the rain and cloudy weather.

They asked about Tommy.

"He dropped off the trail," I told them.

They were disappointed and encouraged me to stick with it. They had told a class of grammar school students about two older men who were hiking the trail, and some of the students had "adopted" Tommy and some had "adopted" me.

With such added incentive, I promised, "I'll try to stick with it."

That night I camped at Curley Maple Gap Shelter.

I met Uncle Johnny the next day. He was the owner of a hiker hostel on the trail at the Nolichucky River in Erwin, Tennessee. Hikers were hanging out, resting and eating at the tables set up in front of the hostel office. A small store next to the office offered hikers the opportunity to stock up on ramen, candy bars, oatmeal, granolas and soft drinks. Toilets and showers were in the back. I looked over the rooms, also out in the back, where hikers had their packs drying in the sun. It was too early to stop for the day; I said goodbye to the delicious accommodations and pushed on.

I had a good cell phone signal and called Tommy and told him about Uncle Johnny's place. Also I told him about yesterday's rain, and he proclaimed, "How glad I am that I no longer have to worry about that. I feel free, at last." He still sounded like a runaway slave.

I stopped at No Business Knob Shelter and read some of the shelter log entries. Three thru-hikers had written about how some day-hikers had hogged the shelter one night and caused them to sleep out in the rain.

Oh, well, I thought, such stuff happens.

Around 8:00 p.m. I set up my tent on some high ridge, cooked supper by headlamp and slept soundly. Off bright and early in the morning, I met a north-bounder, whose trail name was Fed-Ex, a fast hiker who I estimated was in his thirties. He told me he had heard reports of bear activity in the area of High Rocks, where I had camped the night before and had slept blissfully ignorant of the mother and cub that supposedly were foraging for food there.

At noon I took a lunch break at Bald Mountain Shelter and called my wife Jane on my cell. It had been raining most of the morning, and the shelter afforded relief from the rain. After our conversation I moved ahead in the rain and came upon an unexpected piece of Trail Magic about three miles later.

Someone had left a cooler full of cup cakes, cookies, hot coffee and plastic cups for thru-hikers. In the cold rain, nothing was more welcome, especially the fact that someone had thought about hikers on a dreary day. Tears came into my eyes as I experienced the kindness. I wanted to linger on, but I had to reach Sams Gap and the Isuzu before dark.

I made it by 6:00 p.m.

Going on a tip from a northbound hiker who had been treated well there, I drove to the Super 8 Motel in Erwin, Tennessee, where I received a hiker's rate for a room. With a good night's sleep, I arose well rested, put a good breakfast under my belt and ordered two cheeseburgers to take with me on the trail. Then I drove to a point three miles east of Roan Mountain, Tennessee and parked where US 19 E crosses the trail.

I set off in the early afternoon. Along the way I encountered No Pain, a hiker coming north. He was wrapped up in his thermal and wind gear, and he warned me to stay wrapped up in mine. I was grateful for the information when I was greeted by strong, cool winds and overcast skies as I climbed up to the open bald of Hump Mountain. I was to meet No Pain several more times all the way up to Maryland. He had done the trail several times over the past five years.

Two other hikers warned me of the winds. The wind was almost unbearable, and I was glad to finally get down into the trees again. When I arrived at the Overmountain Shelter, I spent the night. There were about twenty other hikers, all of them getting out of the wind.

One of the hikers noted how I had hung my food bag in a tree. It was too close to the trunk, he told me, and he hung it up with his, well over ten feet away from the trunk.

In fact, I was carrying the wrong kind of gear for a food bag and was using a cord that was too heavy. I later bought a spool of twine from a hardware store, and the twine proved to be better for suspending my food bag. I used it from then on for hanging food.

Meanwhile, lucky me, I had my two cheeseburgers for supper.

A girl hiker noted my cheeseburgers and suggested, "That's like cheating."

I didn't argue. I just relished my cheeseburgers, slept well that night and awoke to a beautiful new day.

The dark, cloudy, windy yesterday was replaced by sunshine and expansive views. At Carver's Gap I followed the trail up an abandoned Forest Service road, which made the ascent of Roan Mountain from the north surprisingly easy. But the descent south from the top of Roan Mountain was steep and treacherous. It was hard descending, but I really felt sorry for the north-bounders I met who had to climb.

At Ash Gap I took a two-tenths of a mile side trail to refill my water bottles. I was tempted to put up my tent, but it was too early. I hurried on.

At Hughes Gap I met a friendly red-headed hiker who had run out of water. He was facing a steep climb north, so I gave him one of my water bottles and told him about the water and campsite at Ash Gap, two miles away.

With that in mind, he said he planned to stop at Ash Gap for camping and new water.

I hiked on to Clyde Smith Shelter, refilled my water bottles and looked up to see Fed-Ex, who obliged me by hanging my food bag using his special technique. That night Fed-Ex talked with young hikers about plans to do twenty miles the next day. I listened and envied them for their youth and strength.

I set off in the morning with renewed determination and reached Iron Mountain Gap by noon.

I drove the Buick to Roan Mountain, Tennessee and ate a large barbecue sandwich at a barbecue restaurant. In Roan Mountain my cell had a good signal; I saw that Jane had called and missed me several times. I called and found that Jane and my daughter Karen were the very next day coming into the vicinity of Roan Mountain on the way back from Nashville, where they had attended the funeral of Jane's aunt. We decided to meet at a convenient place in northeastern Tennessee.

I drove to I-81 and took the exit to Kingsport, where I got a motel room for the night and the next day met them at the motel for lunch. Jane thought I looked unchanged by my hike, but Karen thought I had lost weight.

Our unexpected reunion was too short. I waved them away and stayed at the motel another day and took a zero. It was in Kingsport that I bought the spool of twine to use to hang my food bag.

That job done, I began considering how Jane was holding up with my absence from home. She actually supported my doing the hike because I had talked about it for years. She was into Tommy joining me and had hopes that we would go as far as we could.

But Jane had no intention of hiking herself. She has knee problems and even short bike rides set off knee pains and swellings. So we both knew that, when I left, she would assume new responsibilities at home, including many that caused anxiety. The bill paying was relatively easy but dealing with the IRS and with repairing the air conditioner were not easy. Already she had to mail me the tax folder that I used to settle with the IRS at Tommy's cabin. We often talked by phone about those matters, and once she told me that my leaving her in charge was a "shocking act of boldness" on my part.

I asked her directly, "Do you want me to come home?"

To my great relief she did not want me to come home, saying, "I want you to complete the hike."

So I happily continued.

Because of recurrence of back pain (Was it the motel bed or was it yoga practice at the motel?), I decided to take a shorter thirty-five-mile section of the trail on next. I parked my car where US 321 crosses close to Hampton, Tennessee and started hiking the next day.

After steep ups and downs, I put up a tent in a beautiful spot along Laurel Fork, close to USFS 50.

The next day I met Becca at Moreland Gap Shelter. Becca was eating lunch and taking a break.

I stopped and did the same.

She had remembered some of my entries in shelter logs south under the trail name Slow and Steady. She had not taken a zero since Fontana and was looking forward to staying at a hostel on USFS 50, close to where I had tented out. Becca appeared to be in her thirties. She was from Alabama and was hiking alone but was later to have a British fellow join her. I met them several times up through southern Virginia, but they were so fast I soon fell behind them.

At the end of the day I came to Mountaineer Falls Shelter. I shared the shelter with a young German couple who were the only other occupants. They were doing sections of the trail every year and had hiked in New Hampshire a year earlier.

On the third day I made it to the Isuzu on US 19E close to Roan Mountain, Tennessee. I returned to US 321 and swapped the Isuzu for the Buick and took a room at the Howard Johnson in Bristol, Virginia. That night I ate heartily at a KFC buffet on the Tennessee side of Bristol, just across from the motel.

When I returned to the trail the next day I spotted a young male-female pair of hikers thumbing a ride at the exit off I-81 to Damascus, Virginia. They had taken a motel room the night before and were returning to the trail, like me. I stopped and helped them get their backpacks into the trunk — my back seat was already packed with backup hiking gear. They recognized me from the night I spent at Overmountain Shelter. They were getting back on the trail at Damascus to hike north. I had fallen behind them and was going to Damascus to hike south. I let them out at an outfitter's shop and never saw them again.

I drove the Buick to a public lot adjacent to a park in the south end of town and hiked south. After two hours of climbing I arrived at a rolling ridge and made good time but had to stop for a water refill at Abingdon Gap Shelter. The spring was far down off the trail, and it took time.

Several hours were left of daylight, and the shelter was full, so I kept going for another mile and came to a small, two man shelter. I had it to myself, and I put in for the night.

Soon Becca came hiking by. She had put in twenty-three miles that day, but wanted to get to Abingdon Gap Shelter for the night. She waved and kept on going.

Later, after I had gotten into my sleeping bag, two hikers came in and shined their headlamps into the small shelter.

I shined my lamp back and said, "You have one mile to go to reach Abingdon Gap, but there's room for you here — if you care to stay."

Like Becca, they wanted to push on.

The next morning I read the shelter log. Hike On had been there a week earlier. I had last seen him at Flint Mountain Shelter, just before Tommy and I had gone up Big Butt.

The next day I hiked fifteen miles to Iron Mountain Shelter. I t was 6:00 p.m. and the shelter was full, and young thru-hikers had already pitched their tents. I was tempted to go farther, but there was security at these shelters. I decided to stop for the night and put up my tent.

I hung my food bag in a tree, and an older woman — out of sympathy, I think — told me I could hang it in the shelter.

Quite diplomatically I responded, "It's bears, not mice, I'm interested in avoiding. If a bear really wants the food, he'll get at it in a shelter."

The next day I encountered Mountain Lion, an older hiker, at the Vandeventer Shelter. He was resting, exhausted and out of water. I gave him a bottle of my precious water. The water for the shelter was a steep downhill hike, three-tenths of a mile away. Neither of us had the stomach for such a long, downhill excursion.

Later I met Scout with a male companion. I told her she was close to the Vandeventer Shelter. Ten minutes later I met Harvest and explained that Scout was only about ten minutes ahead.

Harvest laughed and said, "We did some partying last night at Watauga Lake Shelter and got a late start this morning."

I descended to Watauga Lake and managed to completely miss the turnoff to the Watauga Lake Shelter. But I did reach the Isuzu at US 321 and drove back to the Howard Johnson in Abingdon, Virginia. I again took in the KFC buffet.

After swapping the Isuzu for the Buick in Damascus, I parked the Buick at Dickey Gap on VA 16.

I made good hiking time and late in the afternoon came onto a big Trail Magic party where VA 603 crosses. A thru-hiker from 2007 had put up coolers of beer, soft drinks, power bars and potato chips, and hikers were invited to partake. I remember there were about ten or more hikers sitting around eating and drinking.

A mellow mood prevailed over the whole gathering. Some were exchanging joints. I recognized a number of hikers but did not know their trail names. I shook hands with the host and was invited to enjoy the food. I took him at his word and enjoyed the soft drinks, granolas and chips. Then I picked up a sixteen-ounce Budweiser, put it in my pack and, after thanking the host again, pushed on to Old Orchard Shelter. I pitched my tent and drank my can of beer. I slept well. It had been a good day.

I had first met Rock-a-Mimi on the balds north of Overmountain Shelter in North Carolina, close to Roan Mountain, where the cold winds had made hiking so difficult. She had warned me to bundle up and secure my hat, but I hardly needed any urging. I met her again the next day when I got into Grayson Highlands State Park.

We stopped and chatted. She had resigned from a job and was hiking the trail. A female hiking companion of hers had to return home after completing her allotted two weeks away from her job, and now Rock-a-Mimi was on her own. She was in her mid-fifties, or so I estimated. We wished each other good luck, and I hiked on to Thomas Knob Shelter.

At Thomas Knob I cooked an early supper and met two young hikers. She was an Obama campaign worker in North Carolina and he was a Duke University Divinity student who had grown weary of the judgmental religion of his Baptist minister father. He was into Buddhist theology and was happy for the change.

She noted how both of their conservative families had slandered Obama and had accused Obama's wife of being unpatriotic. (Michelle had said some things that had been taken out of context.) I sympathized with them politically and theologically. They were going to Mount Rogers, and I wished them the best.

After refilling my water bottles at a fenced-off spot below the shelter (the park's wild ponies have to be fenced out to keep them from soiling the shelter's spring), I resumed hiking. Two miles later I came to a level site next to the trail and pitched my tent for the night.

Becca came hiking by and was followed soon afterward by her male companion and British hiker, Toggle.

That night it rained and the GORP (good old raisins and peanuts) in my food bag was saturated with rain — and spoiled. I tried to dry out the GORP the next morning but without much success. So, I ate as much of it as I could to reduce a heavy, wet load. Near the end of the day I cooked an early supper at Lost Mountain Shelter, taking advantage of a table and seat that made cooking easier. Then I pushed on for two more miles and found a tenting site under the pines close to VA 728. I slept well but heard vehicles off and on all night.

From there, I hiked the last thirteen miles down into Damascus. Some of the time the trail was easy, especially along the Virginia Creeper Trail. For four dollars I took a bunk at The Place, a hiker hostel run by the Methodist Church. That night I had two large hot dogs and a grilled chicken sandwich along with three beers at Dot's Inn Restaurant. What a pleasure it was!

I started the next day at the Cowboy Café with scrambled eggs, bacon, toast and coffee. I then drove the Isuzu to the Relax Inn just off I-81 at Groseclose, Virginia and took a zero day. I saw a number of hikers I had met earlier. Hikers seem to be the main customers at the Relax Inn in late May.

Come morning I had breakfast at a diner. I parked the truck, set off southward and soon met Rock-a-Mimi, who was headed for the Relax Inn. I hiked up and onto a ridge and looked back to the distant I-81: the tiny eighteen-wheelers couldn't be heard now. I pushed on to Partnership Shelter at the Mount Rogers National Recreation Area Center, where I met Mountain Lion again.

I was eager to hurry on for two more miles to reduce my hiking the next day. But after only one mile it began to thunder, and I quickly put up my tent and hung the food bag. The rain held off — until I was about to leave at 6:30 the following morning.

I quickly took down the tent, retrieved my food bag and hiked on, covered up against the rain.

Along the way I met Scout and a male companion. They were planning to stop at Partnership Shelter and order a pizza. Later I met Harvest, who was alone; she was taking a lunch break at an abandoned old school bus pulled up onto a farm next to the trail.

I reached the Buick at Dickey Gap around 4:00 p.m. and drove to the Super Eight Motel at Wyethville, Virginia, where I relaxed, showered, washed clothes and ate real food.

My next section of the trail began where VA 608 crosses the trail close to Crandon, Virginia. I parked the Buick there and began a cloudless day of hiking.

I met Becca as I was passing Helveys Mill Shelter, then I met Toggles, then another girl I had met several times on the trail as well as at the Relax Inn. They were all going so fast that I never saw any of them again.

I refilled my water at Kimberling Creek and crossed I-77, as well as US 52/21, and managed to climb up into the hills above. It was getting late, and close to the trail I found an abandoned forest road flat enough to tent on, though it was a challenge sliding down to it and climbing out the next morning.

On the trail again I met Rock-a-Mimi once more, close to Jenkins Shelter. Water had been an issue all day, and we exchanged information about water sources both north and south of where we were. I was able to get water where she told me it would be, and about a mile later I found yet another water source.

Approximately two miles farther south, I found myself reporting to a young couple about the second source of water. Then I tented out on the mountain side, too weary to journey on as the day came to a close.

I continued to be concerned about water during my hike the following day. I had been correctly warned by the young couple I had met that there would be none until I reached Walker Gap — after a five-mile walk on a rocky ridge line.

A lengthy search revealed water at Walker Gap, which turned out to be a piped spring. I then met three young hikers, including the sexy Downtown Venus, a young woman in her mid-twenties. I told them where to get water, thereby saving them the search I had endured.

Around 4:00 p.m. I reached Chestnut Knob Shelter. There I met Scout and Harvest, Mountain Lion, Day Walker and Alaska, a young hiker with her dog Buddy. The wind was strong, and rain had been predicted. I let Harvest talk me in to staying there for the night. It turned out all three of us old men (me, Mountain Lion and Day Walker) were sixty-three years old. The last two hikers had doctored the spring to make it flow better through a pipe, so we all were able to get water more easily. It did not rain that night as predicted, but I was happy to sleep in the stone shelter.

Harvest told me she had seen the Isuzu two days back. She and Scout had learned to recognize both my vehicles. The three of us were entertained by reading the shelter log entries of hikers, one of whom accused some hikers from Ohio of stealing his umbrella in Hot Springs, North Carolina. Other hikers had written notes exonerating the Ohio boys and saying the accusation was wrong; the Ohio guys were great to be around.

The next morning I rose early and quietly left the shelter. The three young women were still sleeping. I hiked until dusk. I tented out on a flat spot going up Big Walker Mountain. I made an error, pitching my tent on a tree root, and had to reposition myself throughout the night to stay comfortable. But never mind, it rained hard all night long. My tent did not fail me; it kept me cozy and dry, and I was thankful for that.

The next day it was only eight miles to the Isuzu at VA 617. I hurried right along, and when I arrived I drove to the Plaza Motel in Pearisburg, Virginia. I ate a buffet supper at a Chinese café. Other hikers were heartily eating there too. I knew some of them, and we exchanged greetings.

Back on the trail the next day, I parked the Isuzu at the bridge over New River on US 460 and set off south. At the end of the day I met Scout and Harvest at Big Horse Gap. Scout was especially troubled by swarming gnats throughout the day.

A mile later I was up on a beautiful peak and pitched my tent next to a radar station.

The following day I hiked eighteen miles to the Buick at VA 608. That night I was back at the Plaza Motel in Pearisburg, Virginia.

My next section was where VA 42 crosses the trail in Sinking Creek Valley, forty miles north of Pearisburg. It was early June and the heat, gnats and lack of water were starting to be real challenges. I put in ten miles the first day and tented out on top of a ridge close to Lone Pine Peak.

That night two hikers passed by with headlamps, one at midnight and one at 2:00 a.m. They were probably hiking at night to avoid the heat.

The next day I made it to Pine Swamp Branch Shelter and refilled my water bottles. Then I tented out on the ridge above it.

A long day was ahead of me when I got up. Two water sources were dry, but I was able to refill my water at a campsite two miles north of Rice Field Shelter. From a hike three years earlier I knew to use that spring instead of the spring behind the shelter — a tough hike far down below. I arrived at the bridge over New River, where US 460 crosses, and found the Isuzu — missing.

I couldn't believe my eyes!

In the heat I hiked the extra mile up to Pearisburg and got a room at Holiday Motor Lodge. It was the only twenty-mile day of my entire time on the trail, but I had a mission.

I called the police about the Isuzu and learned it had been towed and was told to which shop it had been taken. That was a relief. I could be happy to be at a motel and off the trail. It was Sunday, and the Chinese buffet was available. I ate my fill and then some.

I awoke from a good night's sleep on a full stomach for a change. I called the shop where the Isuzu was supposed to be. They confirmed the truck was there and had been for two days when the police had called them; they considered it an abandoned vehicle. However, the shop owner did admit, "There are four new tires on it as well as a spare, and hiking gear is visible in the cab."

I said, "I parked next to the trail where others had parked. Better parking sites were down close to the river where people fished, but the site I used looked just as good as many other sites along the trail."

His response was, "Come on down, and we'll settle the matter." He followed up with directions.

In the end I paid him a hundred bucks in ransom to get the truck back!

Afterward, I telephoned Tommy about the event. He was convinced the police were running a racket and urged me to cancel the check. I didn't want further problems; I just listened and decided to take more precautions in the future, such as leaving signs in the windows of each vehicle that read the hiker would return to get it.

It was now June 8, 2008. During the past month without Tommy I had added over 300 miles. In fact, I had completed a total of 664 miles, and, despite the heat and water problems, I was feeling strong.

I chose to spend an extra day at the Holiday Motor Lodge and looked forward to more Chinese food.

Restorative measures like rest and large amounts of real food seemed to be keys to staying on the trail for me.

Chapter 5

Ending the Southern Half

June 10, 2008 to July 18, 2008

I next faced a two-day, twenty-mile section from VA 620 at Trout Creek to VA 42 in Sinking Creek Valley. I left the Buick in a shaded parking space at Trout Creek with a visible, handwritten sign that stated the vehicle was not abandoned and that I would soon return.

The day was hot, gnats were swarming and caterpillars were hanging thickly from silk strings along the trail. That night I heard continuous, light pattering sounds on my tent and in the leaves. Upon investigation in the morning, I discovered caterpillars were either falling off their silk strings or defecating.

I pulled everything together after a light breakfast and hiked on. I met an exhausted Rock-a-Mimi, who seemed to have reached her limit from the heat. Later, at Sarver Hollow Shelter, I read a note in the shelter log in which Rock-a-Mimi complained about the heat, the rocky trail and the droppings of the caterpillars. I neither saw her again nor read any of her entries in shelter logs after that day. She must have dropped off the trail.

I reached the Isuzu on VA 42, and, to my relief it, had not been towed.

I spent the night at the Howard Johnson in Cloverdale, Virginia. They allowed me to leave the Isuzu in their parking lot while I returned to the trail for a thirty-three-mile hike back to VA 620.

At Angel's Gap I met three Canadian women, two beautiful young sisters in their early twenties and their very attractive mother, who appeared to be in her early forties. They were strong hikers and pushed right on northward.

That night I tented out with Lemon Drop Bob at Lambert's Meadow campsite. He was doing a section hike for two weeks.

During the night deer came up to the campsite, smelled around us and looked at us, unafraid. Lemon Drop said that they were trying to find salt. Further, during the night I heard frequent stepping sounds around the campsite with pauses next to my tent. Such happenings while inside the tent always freaked me out: I thought of bears. In the morning, Lemon Drop and I were safe and sound. Still, I had to get going quickly — mosquitoes were swarming everywhere.

Toward evening I reached VA 311, where Scout shouted out a greeting. She and two male hikers were being picked up at the trailhead for a trip to town. I went on up the mountain and pitched my tent on the ridge above the road. The morning after, I hiked through cow pastures to find a free-flowing creek.

AT guidebooks advised against drinking from cow pasture streams, but I was to climb the infamous Dragon's Tooth that day and couldn't risk it without water. I finally got water from a creek and treated it with iodine. (I always treated my water with iodine, since

I dislike the flavor of chlorine tablets. I never had giardia or diarrhea on the trail.)

The two-mile climb up Dragon's Tooth was tough, and I was in no mood to take a quarter-mile side trail to the lookout. I reached my Buick at VA 620 and drove back to the Howard Johnson at Cloverdale, where I spent the night. The Isuzu was where I had left it, undisturbed.

After a good night's sleep, I drove to where VA 614 crosses the trail at Jenning's Creek and started the twenty-nine-mile hike back to Cloverdale. I reached the side trail to Bobblets Gap Shelter. I had filled up my water bottles three miles back at Bearwallow Gap, where VA 43 crosses the trail. But the day was hot and I had used two of my four bottles, so I decided to go down the quarter-mile descent to the shelter for more water.

There I met the attractive Downtown Venus again. She and several male hikers were at the shelter. The spring I remembered from my section hike in 2004 was dry, and they told me where to look for water: down a hill behind the shelter. I reached the site but the water flowed in such a slow trickle that after one bottle I did not even try to fill the second. I returned to the shelter and exchanged a few words with the others.

One of the young men I was to meet again in Maine on top of Old Blue Mountain. He said that, after I had left Bobblets Gap Shelter, another man told of how I was doing the trail with two cars, that I was parking north and hiking south and that was why they were always meeting me over and over and why I was always hiking south when meeting these north-bounders. He thought it was cool to hike the trail that way, and he remembered my name and the Bobblets Gap Shelter meeting and told me about it when we met again on Old Blue Mountain in Maine.

I well remembered Downtown Venus and getting water and meeting several male hikers at Bobblets Gap Shelter. I did not remember his name or face, but I pretended that I did when we met again. He was just one of numerous young, fast hikers who made it to Maine.

That night I pitched my tent somewhere close to the Blue Ridge Parkway.

The next day I found good water at Wilson Creek and camped at Fullhardt Knob Shelter. The gnats were too troublesome for me to attempt to sleep in the shelter. I was alone that night and put notes in the shelter log about where to get water for all the north-bounders who might read it. I also wrote about an abandoned backpack with women's clothes and food about two miles north of the shelter. (Later, Harvest saw the abandoned pack and concluded that a girl had probably dropped it there after she had gotten tired of the trail.)

The next day, just out of Cloverdale, I encountered the Canadian women, as well as a red-shirted British-Indian hiker who I had already met a number of times. In Cloverdale I took a room at the Howard Johnson. There I found Scout and Harvest relaxing in the pool. That night they planned to eat at a pizza place across the road, so I didn't need to offer them a ride anywhere.

Most hikers try to be useful to fellow hikers, and I have regretted that I was never able to assist Scout or Harvest with slack packing or rides into town. I helped others but, regrettably, not them.

The next section was from where US 501 crosses the trail at the James River. From there it is about thirty miles back to VA 614 at Jennings Creek.

I don't remember where I tented the first night, but I awoke very concerned about water. A north-bounder had told me that the spring at Thunder Hill Shelter was sluggish, and it was on my mind.

Nonetheless, I found the spring there to be good and later got more water at Cornelius Creek Shelter.

Having put my water worries behind me for the time being, I decided to spend the night at Cornelius Creek Shelter. That is where I met The Mayor and his dog Boll Weevil. The Mayor was so named because his last name sounded sort of like Guilliani, the New York mayor during 9/11. He complimented me for writing about water sources in the shelter logs; he had found my information especially useful when he left Fullhardt Knob Shelter going north. Later, Scout and Harvest came in for the night and tented out behind the shelter.

I slept in the shelter that night with one of the hikers who, along with me and Tommy, lost his food to the bear that night at Walnut Mountain Shelter in North Carolina. Thus we had a common memory of the trail, and it was pleasant to talk about it.

I arrived at Bryant Ridge Shelter the next day. Three years earlier I had slept in that shelter, and the creek was flowing strongly. But today it was almost dry. I did manage to get water from the creek; still, it was mighty slow going.

I made it back to the vehicle at VA 614 and drove to the Budget Inn in Buena Vista, VA on US 60. I booked two nights and took a zero. I wasn't hiking the miles that I had been. Instead of doing fifteen miles a day, I was doing more like ten miles a day; in fact, I had done 110 miles in eleven days. I was hardened as a hiker, but, at age sixty-three, I was not recovering quickly like the younger hikers. I was at my limit and needed rest. You can bet I ate a lot of fast food and drank beer at night and washed my clothes — all of which restored my energy.

After my zero day I was back on the trail at the Tye River, where VA 56 crosses the trail. I climbed up the Priest, a mountain with a bad reputation, but I made it just fine. The ascent was long but seemed to be gradual enough.

I pushed on to Seeley-Woodworth Shelter, which was filled with a number of young women hikers and the young British-Indian man in the red shirt. I pitched my tent just behind the shelter and got under cover just in time for a welcome rain.

The day afterward I saw my first bear, a 200-pound teenager that ran off into the woods and disappeared in a flash.

Then I met Scout and Harvest again. They were upset by "an opinion" that a Trail Angel had expressed; he was dispensing soft drinks and food and free advice to all hikers at a road crossing to the south and told them they were hiking too slowly to make it to Katahdin by the deadline of October 15. (He had jogged the trail several years earlier.) Harvest was especially offended by his opinion of how "slow" she was hiking the trial.

For my own part I considered myself too slow to make Katahdin by the deadline. Anyway, I had already planned to flip-flop in late July up to Maine and proceed south from Katahdin. Tommy had agreed to fly up and help me move the vehicles up north and then fly back to Georgia.

The girls were faster than I was, but they did so many zeroes they were not making progress northward any faster than I was. So, I told them I was planning to flip-flop and they were welcome to do so with me. But they intended to keep going north in an uninterrupted hike.

We talked about some other hikers. From Harvest I learned the British Indian in the red shirt carried a seven-pound rock around in his pack just to prove he could take on the extra weight. (Me? I was always looking for ways to cut weight on my twenty-five-pound pack and lamented the weight of extra water bottles I had to carry because of the drying springs.) Later, in New Hampshire, I met the British Indian and asked him about the rock. By his amused reaction to the story, I suspected it was not accurate, but he did not deny it.

Another hiker heard us talking and pointed out that *real* men carry ten-pound rocks or heavier. I vowed to give the British Indian a new trail name: Rock-man.

That day I made it to Brown Mountain Creek Shelter. The water was good at Brown Mountain Creek. I met Alaska again and her dog Buddy; they had camped out down at the creek. (Alaska and Buddy were to be important later when I flip-flopped up to Maine.)

The next day I met The Mayor and Boll Weevil at the Pedlar River, where I took a lunch break. Boll Weevil jumped in the river and had a great time. We talked about how Harvest had been offended by the jogger's opinion about her slowness. He had been at the road crossing where the encounter occurred and did not find the jogger as offensive as Harvest had.

I came upon Rainbow and her dogs on a ridge the next day. She and some male hikers had come up from the valley that morning.

I reached my car at US 501 and drove back to Buena Vista for a night in the Budget Inn. After some good food and a night's rest, I drove to Rockfish Gap, where US 250 and I-64 cross the trail, and parked the Buick.

I started south and, to my amazement, I met a young couple I had last seen at Brown Mountain Creek Shelter. They were moving swiftly ahead, but that was for the "young." I never saw that couple again.

I next pitched my tent in a gap on a ridge north of Humpback Mountain and was soon joined by Camel, a lone hiker in his fifties. That night we provided each other with psychological security out on the remote ridge. As a comforting measure, no doubt, he called family members on his cell phone. Meanwhile, I broke a support rod as I was setting up my tent for the night, but the tent stood up well enough, and I was glad for the protection.

As I moved out and onward in the morning, I met Calvin and Hollywood coming up to the peak of Humpback Mountain. They were an intelligent, friendly male/female duo. I estimated them to be in their mid-thirties. I had seen them earlier, north of Cloverdale and along the Blue Ridge Parkway. Like The Mayor, they found my information about water sources useful and were kind enough to say so. They were faster than I was, and it proved to be the last time I would see them face to face. But I did read some of their entries in hiker logs up north.

I reached Maupin Field Shelter and met Poet and Hippie Chick, a husband and wife team. They were soon off to the north.

After cooking and eating a freeze-dried supper and refilling my water supply, I was off to the south and tented out at Bee Mountain. When I heard Alaska and Buddy walk by, I just kept to my tent and did not call out. It was dark already, and I might scare her, I reasoned. But the unvarnished truth was that I was just too tired to interact.

The day after I made it up both the Three Ridges and the Chimney Rocks and down to Harpers Creek Shelter. Four years earlier I had almost died from dehydration when I tried this section without enough water and without being in hiking condition. This time it was much easier — not a piece of cake, but I was in no danger of dying. I made it to my car on the Tye River and traveled the road to Waynesboro, Virginia, where I took a motel room.

I had been out only seven straight days and had done seventy-seven miles. With that under my belt, I decided I deserved a zero the next day. I ate well and washed clothes again. And I swapped my broken tent poles for Tommy's good tent poles, which I had kept in my car after Tommy's departure. I mailed the broken poles to Tommy, who mailed them back to Big Agnes in Colorado and got Big Agnes to send a replacement set to his home in Georgia.

My next section of the AT was forty-five miles from where US 33 goes under Skyline Drive in the Shenandoah down to Rockfish Gap. I stopped at Hightop Hut for a rest and met Bingo Pajamas and her male companion. I took photos of them; I was now carrying my camera to get a picture of my dear Harvest and Scout, who I would soon leave because of my plan to flip-flop up to Maine.

I pushed on and came to Pinefield Hut, which was full of hikers playing cards. I tented out behind the shelter. Later Camel, Hippie Chick and Poet came in, and they too tented out.

Shenandoah National Park provided tall, metal poles with hooks on top so hikers can hang up food away from bears. You have to hoist your bag on the end of a metal rod and maneuver it onto one of four hooks at the top of the tall pole. No bear can get up slick poles, which are just as secure as the bear cables in Georgia and in parts of the Smokies.

That night we heard heavy foot falls and snuffling, and in the morning Poet swore a large bear was just outside the tent in which he and his wife Hippie Chick were sleeping. He also admitted that he did not look out to confirm his suspicions. He said he was ready to jab it with his hiking pole if it invaded his tent.

The deer had been all around before we went to sleep, and it could be that, in his mind, he exaggerated their noises into bear-like noises. Deep inside our tents we knew that we had very little protection if a bear really wanted to get us.

Since we were all safe and well in the morning, I pushed on to Blackrock Hut to fill up my water supplies. I found a number of hikers hanging out at the hut. Wolfman made a sandwich for me with a big, juicy wiener topped with tomato and mustard. What a delight! It was well worth the two-tenths of a mile descent to the hut. I took his picture along with some other hiker and hurried on. I made it back to my car at Rockfish Gap and spent the next night in a motel in Waynesboro.

On July 3, after a late start, I drove to where US 522 crosses the trail just north of Shenandoah National Park and parked the Isuzu. I climbed up into the park and registered at a self-register kiosk. By the end of the day I passed North Marshall Mountain and set up my tent. After supper I began looking for a tree to hang my food bag and saw a large black bear passing by on the trail about forty feet away from my tent.

I stood stark still, determined not to display any fear or weakness. I had read that you should look as big as you can and never run.

The bear stopped and looked back at me.

I raised my two hiking poles and made a step toward him.

It ran around a tree and hissed back at me.

I then turned down the trail in the opposite direction and found a tree to hang up my food, always keeping an eye out for the bear. I did not want it to follow me, and I didn't see it again. I considered taking down my tent and moving on, but I was too tired and stayed where I was. I slept that night with my hiking poles inside the tent, ready to poke the bear if he tried to molest me.

I was off and hiking at sunrise, to reduce the chance of encountering that bear again. I hiked down to Gravel Springs Hut to get water and use the privy. I read the hut log about how two young bears had climbed trees around the hut and had been hanging out looking for food. Later that day I saw a cub scamper across the trail and disappear into the woods. I knew the mother must be close by, but I didn't see her.

I later encountered The Mayor and Boll Weevil taking a break at a lookout. He told me he and Rainbow would soon flip up into Pennsylvania and would not be able to take me up on my offer to flip him up to Maine. I soon met Rainbow and her two dogs and got their photos, and at some point I met Alaska and her dog Buddy. I told her about my plans to flip-flop up to Maine, and she said she was interested in flip-flopping if I had room. She gave me her cell phone

Alaska and her dog Buddy on the trail.

number, and I promised I would call her when Tommy came up to help me drive the two vehicles.

The rains came as I stopped at Elkwallow Wayside for hot dogs and snacks.

I hiked on and passed a shelter on the trail where I met a forty-five-year-old man from Ohio who was on the trail for the first time.

He had been out for a few days and was going slowly at about six miles a day. He was having trouble, and the only cure for him was to get into hiking condition. I gave him some encouraging words.

I cooked supper and went on up a mountain and got my tent pitched just before the rains cut loose again. I stayed dry and snug, and I was thankful for my excellent, lightweight tent.

Over three days I made the next forty miles and tented on ridge tops twice. I found that the easy miles that the Shenandoah section of the trail was supposed to offer were not that easy. Instead, there were rocky sections with many ascents.

I reached the Buick at US 33 and drove in the rain to a motel at Luray, Virginia, where I spent the night. I had hiked 107 miles in eight days, and I decided to take a zero in Luray and to get my Buick a new safety sticker. The current one was to expire the next month.

At the motel where I stayed I met Chip, a fast hiker who was sharing a room with a group of other young hikers. I was resting in my room after a couple of beers when Chip knocked on my door. His group had gotten groceries at Walmart, and they had called Chip on his cell and asked if I could pick them up. So, I cleared out my back seat and went to Walmart where they loaded the groceries into my car. One hiker came back with me to the motel, and he and Chip and I unloaded the groceries into their room. The other hikers stayed at Walmart and the mall.

On July 9, my Buick passed inspection, and I had a new safety sticker for a year.

Now the time had arrived for exchanging the Buick for the Isuzu at US 522. I drove the Isuzu to Snicker's Gap where VA 7 crossed the trail.

I met a hiker who was out of money and had learned that his father in Pennsylvania had been hospitalized with a heart attack. I gave him forty dollars to get transportation home. He also was out of food; I gave him two freeze-dried dinners. I regret forgetting his trail name. He was planning to get lodging at a hostel close to Bear's Den Rocks.

I pitched my tent somewhere on the "roller coaster" section that night. While in my sleeping bag I received a call on my cell phone from someone who wanted to buy the Isuzu. I had left a message in the window about how I would return to the truck after completing a section of the trail and please not tow it off. I had written down my cell number in case there were any problems. I told the inquirer the truck belonged to my nephew and I could not sell it.

The next day at the side trail to Sky Meadows State Park I met Robert Freeman, a Ridgerunner who was performing trail maintenance. I was taking a rest on the rarest of trail luxuries: an actual resting bench. Robert also took a rest on the bench. He loved the trail and had volunteered his services on this northern Virginia section. (I would see Robert at the end of my hike in December at Caledonia State Park in Pennsylvania, where he lives close by.)

I made it back to the Buick and went to a motel in Front Royal for the night.

I next drove to Harpers Ferry National Historic Park Headquarters and parked the Buick in the general parking lot after registering it for a week. I then took the tourist bus down to the historic town of Harpers Ferry and walked back to the trail where it crosses over the Shenandoah River on the US 340 bridge.

I was now in the short West Virginia section.

I had started the hike late and after about eight miles I tented somewhere, I just can't remember precisely where. The next morning

I came to the 1,000-mile marker — that is, 1,000 miles from Springer, the southern terminus of the AT.

The marker is written on the ground with brick-sized stones and is set next to a large boulder.

I came to the Virginia state line; it promised 535 miles of hiking south to Damascus.

As I reached Snickers Gap, heavy rains came. I was drenched. I took refuge in the Isuzu and drove to a motel in Charles Town, West Virginia.

After studying the trail maps I was confident that I could do the Maryland section over the next four days and be ready to pick up Tommy on July 18th at the Baltimore airport. Tommy and I would then drive the vehicles up to Maine.

I drove the Isuzu up to Pen Mar County Park on the Maryland-Pennsylvania border and started hiking south. I missed a turn and got off the trail down a road parallel to a railroad line. I kept cursing the

Pen Mar Park on the Maryland-Pennsylvania Border, the northern end of my hike from Georgia. I left the Isuzu here, hiked southward to Harpers Ferry to get the Buick, then picked up Tommy at the Baltimore Airport.

lack of trail marking "blazes" and attributed it to the lack of funds for the local trail maintenance group.

I finally found some hikers who were clearly not hardened AT hikers. They told me I was off the AT and said I should retrace my steps back toward Pen Mar Park. Sure enough, I came to where I had gone wrong, got back on the trail and found plenty of white blazes to guide me.

After only three miles I met Scout and Harvest close to High Rock. I was thrilled to finally get their pictures. It was the last time I would see them. (We managed to miss each other in New Hampshire; they passed by while I was taking a zero in North Woodstock.) After getting their pictures we had an emotional group hug because I was to

Harvest and the author.

Scout and the author.

flip-flop in a few days, and I feared we might not meet again. Where I spent the night I don't remember. I tented out that night in the woods.

At noon the next day I met Chip from the motel in Luray, Virginia. Chip and his hiking buddy had already done fifteen miles that morning and were planning to do twenty-five more for the day!

I told them they must take care not to injure themselves. They were into the four-state challenge, for which hikers take in four states in one day (Virginia, West Virginia, Maryland and Pennsylvania). They would have to do more than forty miles to accomplish such a crazy feat. So, even if Chip could not do four states in one day, he was planning to do forty miles, which was the same thing. I wished him the best and never saw him again.

At the end of the day I took the I-70 foot-bridge overpass and soon afterward put up my tent.

That night I heard deep hissing or panting sounds. I imagined a big bear, of course, like the one that hissed at me in Shenandoah. It may have been a deer, but I spent a tense hour or more worrying about a bear. Finally, I fell asleep.

Mid-morning of the next day I came to the old, original Washington Monument, a stone edifice put up in 1827 by locals. I got up in the top of the thirty-foot tower and had extensive views all around. A quarter of a mile beyond the monument I was able to get fresh tap water for my bottles and use the public rest room.

I soon came to the old National Turnpike at Turner's Gap, where US A-40 crosses. Within a few hundred yards of the road, there was Dahlgren Back Pack Camping Area, where I read in the logbook that Calvin and Hollywood had been through a week earlier and had taken a shower. I also met No Pain again, the hiker who I had met several times in North Carolina. I got his picture and walked on.

At the end of the day I reached Ed Garvey Shelter, which was full of day hikers. I pitched my tent. No Pain came in later. He was taking the section from north to south, like me. He put up his hammock. During the night I heard many noises that I swore must have been bears; but, in the morning, No Pain claimed it was only deer. He had hiked the trail four times, so I gave him credit for knowing his noises. But it sounded too heavy to me for deer.

I made it back to Harpers Ferry the next day. I bought soft drinks from a wheelchair-bound veteran who was selling his drinks at a point on the C&O Canal Towpath where the Goodloe Byron Memorial Footbridge crosses into Maryland over the Potomac River. He was very friendly, and we talked about my hike and how Tommy had to drop out. He exonerated Tommy, saying something like, "To each his own."

After leaving him, I felt how fortunate I was to have use of my body and how remarkable the crippled veteran was for being able to engage in life discussions with able-bodied people like me and for making his life into something good despite his paralyzed legs.

After crossing over into West Virginia I stopped at the Appalachian Trail Conservancy headquarters in Harpers Ferry and had my picture taken. I registered as a thru-hiker "Flip-Flopper," the forty-seventh one to do so for 2008. Over 600 thru-hiker north-bounders had registered and only a few "pure" south-bounders had registered. I studied the book and found Scout, Harvest, Bones, Becca, Toggle, Camel, Rockman, Downtown Venus, Hike On, the three Canadian women, Calvin and Hollywood. I recognized a number of other hikers I had met, as well.

I returned to the trail and completed the last half mile to the US 340 bridge and backtracked into the old Harpers Ferry town, where I caught the tour bus back to the park headquarters.

I then drove my Buick up to Hagerstown, Maryland and got a room at the Super Eight Motel. The next day was a zero during which I waited for Tommy to come into the Baltimore Airport. I called Alaska and found she and Buddy were at a motel in Front Royal. Shepherd and his dog were with her, and I agreed I would flip-flop all of them in my car the next day.

I was now a hardened hiker with over 1,000 miles behind me. I knew there was strength in my arms and legs that would carry me on, unless I got sick or injured. My arms were strong and muscular because of the constant use of hiking poles. I could even feel the pectoral muscles under my shirt. I was confident that I would not lose my motivation to continue; it was as strong now as in the beginning.

Meanwhile, I had great respect for the other hikers, most of whom were faster than I was, and that included the young women. Despite the inevitable exhaustion at the end of each hiking day, I loved the hiking and loved being part of the hiking community. I only wished Tommy would rejoin me, but he gave me no indication that he would. He would help me flip the vehicles up to Maine, but that was all he promised.

Chapter 6

Getting to and Hiking Maine

July 18, 2008 to September 1, 2008

On July 18 at around 9:00 p.m. I picked up Tommy at the Baltimore airport. My next task was to make it to Pen Mar County Park on the Pennslyania/Maryland border where I had parked the Isuzu. It took a number of false turns, backtracking and even some cursing, but a little after midnight I drove into Pen Mar Park and found the Isuzu undisturbed.

Tommy drove the Isuzu and followed me to the motel in Hagerstown, where we arrived around 1:00 a.m. We enjoyed a good night's sleep and breakfasted at the motel.

Then I called Alaska and asked for the directions and name of her motel in Front Royal, Virginia. I drove the Buick to the motel in Front Royal and picked up Alaska and Shepherd, and their dogs.

Meanwhile, Tommy worked on the Isuzu's blinker light, which had started to malfunction in Buena Vista. He was able to temporarily fix it. That done, Tommy started north on I-81 in the Isuzu. Throughout the day we kept in contact by cell. We made it to the

Atlantic Coast on I-95, stopping at a motel in New Hampshire, where Tommy had called and received approval for the dogs. The next day Alaska called the Econo Lodge in Millinocket, Maine and got an okay to bring the dogs.

In the morning we were back on I-95. We drove up to Medway, Maine, where Tommy had reserved a motel room, while I proceeded on to Millinocket, Maine. I left Alaska, Shepherd and the dogs at the Econo Lodge.

About the dogs — they were well behaved and had not barked or fought. Buddy did have a way of begging. Once, when I was eating a cheeseburger, Buddy was in the front seat and looked longingly into my eyes and at the cheeseburger. I finally gave in and broke off a small piece for him, which he gobbled it up in a snap. A little later I gave him another piece, which he disposed of in the same way. On the whole, the dogs did well. There were no accidents in the car, probably due in part to the frequency with which we visited the rest areas on I-95, where we took them to the dog walking zones to let them take care of business. They did shed hair that I later cleaned up.

Alaska and Shepherd had to have their dogs boarded in Millinocket when they hiked in Baxter Park; dogs were not allowed in the park. After they had hiked to the Katahdin summit they went back to Millinocket to get their dogs and hiked the rest of Maine.

After leaving the Econo Lodge, I drove the ten miles back to Medway where Tommy and I had supper. The next day I decided that we should leave the Isuzu at Arbol Bridge, fifteen miles south of the Katahdin summit. We then took pictures of me and Tommy at the Millinocket city limit sign.

Tommy said he would arrange to have the photos printed in his hometown newspaper. Then we drove the Buick down to Portland,

Maine, and Tommy took a flight back to Georgia. He had been true to his word; he had helped me flip-flop up to Maine, but he was not about to resume hiking with me.

That night I drove back to Millinocket and stayed at the Hotel Terrace. The morning after I drove to Arbol Bridge and parked the Buick next to the Isuzu. I planned a two-day hike up to Katahdin from Arbol Bridge.

The first day was a relatively easy ten miles to Katahdin Stream Campground. I was passed by a group of Explorer Scouts who were able to ford a fast moving stream without getting wet. I forded the stream and fell — and got both boots soaked. Later I was passed by two pretty girls, graduates from one of universities in New England. They were hiking the 100 Mile Wilderness now that they had time off.

When I arrived at the Katahdin Stream Campground, the Scouts were there, as well as the two young women — they were waiting to get tent-site assignments. I had already made reservations for a site and hurried on.

After an all night rain, July 24 was to be five miles up to Katahdin and back. But the weather was bad with such fog and wind that, as I climbed above tree line, I could barely make my way from one rock marker — which I could hardly see or find — to the next. I took the Hunt Trail (same as the AT), which is one of the steepest sections of the entire trail, and got as far as the two-mile marker from the peak. I encountered the Explorer Scouts as they were coming down from the peak. They had made it and were happy to be getting out of the wind and fog. A few of their colleagues had turned back earlier, and I had directed them to shelter in one of the caves halfway up the mountain.

The infamous two-mile mark on Katahdin.

The fog grew even thicker. I had to make a decision about whether to go on in the fog or to stop. If I got lost on the mountain in the fog, and if the fog did not lift for another day, I could run out of food, warmth and life. I went back and forth about it in my mind. I even sat down and waited to see if the fog might lift, but it didn't. I soon started feeling the cold wind. With heavy heart — after much anticipation — I turned back down the mountain.

I regretted my decision; I'd been so close to the end. But bad decisions cost lives, and I didn't want to be one of them. I resigned myself: I would just have to attempt the summit again. I could not be this close to the northern terminus and not accomplish it. I returned to Katahdin Stream Campground and spent a second night. The next day I hiked the ten miles back to Arbol Bridge.

At a motel in Millnocket I studied maps of the trail south of Arbol

Slow and Steady

On the trail in Maine — shows the tendency of tree branches
to grow in one direction, which fascinated the author.

Bridge and called Katahdin Iron Works, a company that owns much of the land through which the trail passes for about eighty miles south of Arbol Bridge. I wanted to park my vehicle on one of their lumber roads and hike back to Arbol Bridge. I was told that all I needed to do to park on their roads was to register at the entrance gates and pay a ten-dollar fee. I registered at the Jo Mary Road entrance off ME 11 then drove up Jo Mary Road and off onto Kokadjo-B Pond Road to where the trail crosses. There I started a forty-seven-mile hike northward.

The first evening I camped at Antlers Campsite. The most notable difference in the hiking, compared to Virginia, was the water. Maine's rainy summer had caused the streams to flow abundantly; in fact, the trail was often flooded, and the insides of my boots were often wet. Also the temperatures were cooler, as low as fifty-five degrees in the morning.

After four days of wet-cool hiking I reached the Buick at Arbol Bridge and drove to Millinocket and the Econo Lodge. I took a zero day at the motel. Later that same day I went to the Baxter State Park Office in Millinocket and reserved a campsite for myself for August 3rd at one of the campgrounds on the back side of Katahdin. Thus, I would be allowed to arrive very early and start hiking up Katahdin from the back side.

Refreshed with food and rest at the Econo Lodge, I returned to the trail on another Katahdin Ironworks Logging Road. I had to ford the West Branch of Pleasant River, and over the next two days I hiked without remembering where I tented.

At one point I met Alaska, Shepherd and their dogs. I was glad to see them, and we talked for a while. They had fared better on their summit at Katahdin. The weather was good for them.

Trudging onward, I reached the Isuzu at Kokadjo-B Pond Road and drove back to Millinocket and the Econo Lodge. I was ready to try the summit again in the morning, and I was hoping this, a day of rain, would go away for a dry hike tomorrow.

I arrived at Baxter State Park at 6:00 a.m. I had to show my permit and reservation, made earlier in Millinocket. I drove to one of the campgrounds on the back side of Katahdin and started hiking early. Water from yesterday's rain was running down the trail in streams. I moved on and reached the Katahdin summit in the early

Triumphant! The author on the summit of Katahdin.

afternoon of August 3. I had my picture made by a group of young-
sters already there

Afterward I paused for a look at the summit, but fog had rolled in
and little could be seen. I shrugged and hiked down to the two-mile
mark on the Hunt Trail (AT) where the fog had stopped me on my
first attempt at the summit ten days earlier. I retraced my steps back
up to Thoreau Spring and took a side trail around the summit and
back down to the campground.

I arrived at the end of the day, and it was getting dark. I decided to
cancel my campground reservation and drove out of the park back to
Millinocket and the Econo Lodge. I could now forget my earlier failed
attempt at the summit. I had hiked it, and I could say as much. Still,
I had thoughts of that "missing mile" I still had to climb at Springer,
since Tommy had refused to do it in March. Hiking 2,175 miles, minus
two miles for Katahdin and one mile for Springer, well, that would not
have been psychologically acceptable to me.

Up and ready to move on the next morning, I drove the Isuzu
down to Monson to pick up eye medication sent by Jane. I then went
to where the trail crosses on ME 15 and parked the truck. I hiked
north as swiftly as I could because it was threatening rain. After a few
miles I stopped at a hostel and spent the night.

I was the only person in the hostel, so there wasn't anything going
on to distract me, and it was there that I discovered my right boot had
a hole in it. No wonder my right foot had felt wet since I'd been on the
trail in Maine! Oh, well . . .

On the following day I had to ford several streams and stopped
for lunch at Wilson Valley Lean-to. Soon after leaving there, I encountered Shepherd, Alaska and their dogs. They were planning to make
it in to Monson that night. I told them about the hostel, and they

talked as if they might do it then warned me about the rough trail over Chairback Mountain.

I made it to Long Pond Stream Lean-to and tented out. The day afterward, I hiked only to Chairback Gap Lean-to, where I slept in the shelter. The third day I went over Chairback Mountain in the rain to find that the descent on the north side was steep and dangerous.

It was like moving down a rock slide; the rain was pouring down and the ground was extremely slippery. Despite everything, I managed to reach the Katahdin Ironworks Logging Road in one piece and found the Buick where I had parked it.

I signed out at one of the back entrances and took the road to Greenville, Maine, where I checked into a motel. Exhausted by the difficult trail, the rains and the wet boot, I took a zero on August 8.

With a day of luxury and eating real food behind me, I retrieved my backup military boots from the Buick, and I was back in business — not a minute too soon. My right foot had been taking a beating, and I blessed my foresight in bringing along the extra pair of boots.

Meanwhile, I realized how slow hiking was for me in Maine. I had completed the summit and the 100 Mile Wilderness, which was not really a wilderness thanks to the roads of Katahdin Ironworks. But I was going at a rate slower than I had in Virginia. The last thirty miles from Monson to my Buick had been done in three and a half days, which was slower than the twelve to fifteen miles a day in Virginia. I didn't know what I could do about it, but the thought crossed my mind: *maybe I need more rest.* I shelved that idea and set forth again.

I started at Caratunk, Maine, where US 201 crosses the trail. I left the Isuzu at the trailhead and set off northward. I tented out close to Pleasant Pond. The day afterward, I hiked as far as Bald Mountain Brook Lean-to and spent the night in the shelter.

The following morning I again met Alaska and Shepherd with the dogs. Alaska warned me about the dangers of fording the east branch of the Piscataquis River and how she had taken an eight-mile road detour around the east and west branches of that river to avoid the high water. She had left a drawing of the detour route in the Moxie Bald Lean-to, where she had stayed the night before.

When I reached the Moxie Bald Lean-to, I studied the detour she had drawn then hurried onward. The water was high after recent rains, and I did not feel safe trying to ford the west branch. So, I took the eight-mile road detour around the swollen Piscataquis River. I knew a number of young hikers had been able to do the fords in spite of the high water, but I just did not feel comfortable trying.

With three miles to go, I was lucky to be helped by a real Trail Angel, one Mrs. Shaw, the owner of Shaw's Boarding House in Monson. Shaw's Boarding House is a haven for weary hikers, and she is accustomed to the peculiarities of hiker subculture. She found me on her way back from delivering a vigorous young man to the trail at the point I had started my eight-mile road detour. He was to jog the trail without a pack and ford the east and west branches of the river in the bargain!

Mrs. Shaw drove me three miles, crossing the bridge over the Piscataquis River and to the trail crossing on Shirley-Blanchard Road. I thanked her and got back on the trail.

Later the young jogger passed me and said he would see me at Shaw's. But I did not go to Shaw's Boarding House; that night I tented beside a lake. The next day I came to the Buick at the trailhead on ME 15, and I drove to a motel in Greenville.

From Greenville, I drove to the trailhead on ME 27, close to Stratton. I hurried back to the trail and climbed into the beautiful

Bigelow Mountains. I got over the western peak and made camp in the Avery Memorial Campsite in Bigelow Col. All of the wooden tenting platforms were taken, so I tented on the ground between two tall evergreens.

Newlyweds were camping on a nearby platform where he had proposed to her a year ago that day. The next morning they were returning to civilization, and when they departed left me some bottled water and food. Off I went . . .

I hiked up to Avery Peak on top of Bigelow Mountain. It was so beautiful I wanted to stay, but I pushed on and tented at Little Bigelow Lean-to. At Little Bigelow Lean-to I readily gave my place to a young woman who hiked without a tent. I preferred the privacy of my own tent to the common sleeping area of the lean-to, so I was happy to let her have my section of the wooden floor. I tented out behind the lean-to. As it turned out, the lean-to that night was filled with hikers — among them were two women, Shady and Crackers.

Trudging onward the following day, I got as far as East Carry Pond.

I pushed off at first light the next day so I could arrive at the Kennebec River Canoe Ferry before 2:00 p.m. The worst of it that morning was to find an unbelievable ford at the mouth of Pierce Pond. I was able to bypass that danger by detouring three-tenths of a mile off to Harrison's Pierce Pond Camps, where a bridge crossed the river that came out at Pierce Pond. In dry weather the ford would have been doable, but it was not doable now — at least not for me. I continued on and did ten miles to the Kennebec River, getting there by noon, well ahead of my 2:00 p.m. deadline.

I had to wait until the Canoe Ferry man returned from lunch. Upon his arrival, he paddled over and I climbed into the canoe and helped him paddle back across. We paddled hard to keep the canoe going upstream. The week earlier he had not operated the ferry for two days because of high water. Today the water was high but had gone down from the past week.

I caught up with the Isuzu at Caratunk and drove to Stratton. I checked into a motel and ate real food that night as well as the next morning. Then I took a rare one-day hike.

I drove the Isuzu to the trailhead on Caribou Valley Road and walked eight miles over Crocker Mountains South and North back to ME 27 where the Buick was located. From there I drove to the White Wolf Inn in Stratton and took a room for a two-day rest. I was still tired from some very rough hiking. Meanwhile, across the street from the White Wolf Inn I found a restaurant and a diner. I took full advantage of them!

Between meals I was resting in my room at the White Wolf when I saw two familiar faces walking past a window — the twins, Danger Snake and Time Cop. Tommy and I had last seem them in North Carolina. I yelled out to them, and they recognized me. I left my room and went out to talk with them.

I offered them a ride back to the trail. While they considered the proposition, I recognized a young woman hiker I had last seen at the Plumorchard Gap Shelter in Georgia. She had slept on the lower level, while Tommy and I had slept on the second level. She did not remember me, but after she and her male companion picked up a package at the post office, they welcomed a ride to the trailhead on ME 27, where I wished them good luck.

Upon my return to the White Wolf the twins had decided to take a zero day at the motel, just like me. I rested the remainder of the day and read. The next morning I got ready to return to the trail, but I first offered to shuttle the twins back. They were contemplating taking a second zero, but decided to return to the trail. I stopped at the ME 27 trailhead and bid farewell to Danger Snake and to Time Cop.

I drove ME 16 to Rangeley, having first picked up a hitchhiker who had just done a section of the trail. He was going back home but was also stopping at the trailhead on ME 4 to pick up his car. I

Rough hiking in Maine, this is typical
of peaks in Maine and New Hampshire.

stopped at an outfitter store and bought a new pair of boots. I continued to the trailhead on ME 4, let the other man off at his car and started hiking north.

I don't remember the details of the twenty-four miles back to the Isuzu, except that the hiking was beautiful and difficult. I do remember when I came to Sugarloaf Mountain Trail. I was pleased the Maine Appalachian Trail Club did not own Sugarloaf Mountain. If they had owned it, they would have routed the trail over it. I was happy to be able to avoid the six-tenths-of-a-mile side trail to the summit of that privately owned mountaintop.

Gosh, but I was tired of climbing up peaks!

One night in my tent I heard loud, stepping noises, probably from a moose. I was not worried about bears so much in Maine as in Virginia, but I still hung my food up with bears in mind.

I recall a steep descent after the trail passed the side trail to Sugarloaf; it was so steep that I had to hang on to boulders and slide down on my bottom to avoid headlong falls.

I also began a string of meetings with two women hikers, Crackers and Shady. I had seen them doing the section north of Stratton, and I must have seen them doing this section south of Stratton, but I can't recall the exact site. I do not remember first meeting them, but Shady asserts that we first met at the Little Bigelow Lean-to where I tented out in the back to make room for the girl hiking without a tent.

I reached the South Branch of the Carrabassett River, and I had to do a balancing act to cross a plank bridge over it. There were two hikers waiting to cross the plank. I did not know what was holding them back — they were younger and stronger than I was. I joked that I had no worries crossing because they were there to fish me out if I fell in. I made it okay, but they were holding back — thinking it over, I guess.

I reached the Caribou Valley Road, and the Isuzu was a welcome sight. I delayed a few minutes in case the other hikers wanted a ride to Stratton, but they never came along. Finally I left and spent the night at a motel in Stratton.

The following morning I drove down to South Arm Road, which crosses the trail nine miles north of Andover, Maine. From the road crossing I hiked the trail northward. I tented out late in the afternoon on Old Blue Mountain. I was joined later by a lone hiker who immediately recognized me. He called me by my trail name and re-counted last seeing me at Bobblets Gap Shelter close to Virginia's Blue Ridge Parkway. He had remembered me because others had talked about how I was using two vehicles to do the trail, and he thought it was an interesting way to do it. He remembered Downtown Venus, who was there at the shelter when I had passed through.

"Who could forget the pretty Downtown Venus?" he said.

I remembered Downtown Venus quite well, but I did not remember him. However, I sort of faked it, and we had a nice conversation.

He had a Big Agnes tent like I had, and he had experienced a break in the support poles in the same place that I had. We tented out side by side that night, and he left early in the morning. I never saw him again. I regret not remembering his name.

I hiked on for another ten miles and tented out on the north side of Bemis Stream at a well used campsite.

The next day I met Crackers and Shady hiking south and told them about the good campsite at Bemis Stream — good campsites on both north and south sides. I encouraged them by saying, "The ford-ing of the stream's easy."

Crackers was in her early fifties. She had recently retired from work as emergency dispatcher in emergency medicine. She had experience in the area of rescue medicine and carried some medi-cations with her, including epinephrine (also known as adrenalin), which I had also been carrying. She had met Shady, who worked at an outfitters' store in North Carolina, and they decided to hike the trail together. They had started late in the season (May), and when they reached Damascus, Virginia they took the Greyhound Bus and flip-flopped up to Maine, and were now hiking south. I kept meeting them because, as I progressed south with two vehicles, I always hiked north, section after section. I was meeting them regularly and took interest in their well being.

I moved on after the last encounter with Shady and Crackers and reached another place to pitch my tent, but I forget where it was. On the fourth day of this period, I arrived at the Buick in the morning and picked up three hikers and drove them to the grocery store in Rangeley. They were able to get bunks at a hiker hostel on Gull Pond. I drove down to Andover, Maine and got a room in the Pine Ellis Hiking Lodge. I took two nights, which allowed me to take a zero the next day. I was exhausted from hiking, and I needed the rest. I think that's why my memory is so bad over that period: it was taking everything I had just to hike.

I really enjoyed resting and eating real food at the nearby country store. That night I met Crackers and Shady at the hostel. They had moved off the trail at a road crossing and had gotten a ride to the hostel. They too were tired. And to cap it off I met Bones again, the young man who Tommy and I helped in North Carolina when he was incapacitated one night with vomiting after eating wild onions.

Bones recognized me while I was talking with my wife Jane on the phone. After I finished my call, he came up to me and renewed old memories. I regret not getting his photo but did not think about it until the next day when it was too late.

When I returned to the trail again, I was able to take Shady and Crackers to Grafton Notch where ME 26 crosses. They were doing a "slack-pack" hike north for ten miles to a crossing on East B Hill Road, where the hostel would send a van to pick them up. Slack packing is when the hiker goes with a light pack: no tent and only one day's worth of food.

I also hiked north but carried a full pack and planned to tent out and follow up the next day with a ten-mile section to the Isuzu on South Arm Road.

Soon they were out of sight; they walked faster than I, even when they were full-packing.

I came to Bald Pate, west and east peaks. These peaks were equal to the Bigelow peaks in beauty. I hated to leave, but I continued on and tented at Dunn Notch and Falls. Actually, signs prohibited camping there, but I set up my tent a quarter mile farther north. That night some frisky small animal ran to my tent repeatedly and a number of times brushed against it. I did not get a look at it, I was just too tired. Whatever it was, it was persistent.

A day followed during which I had to scramble over a rock slide/land slide, about which I had been warned by other hikers. Part of a steep slope had given way. I had to cross on exposed rock with no bushes to hold on to; the soil had slipped down the steep side of a hill. I made it by taking off my pack and sliding it across. If it had been raining, it would have been more dangerous. I was relieved to get it all behind me.

Late in the afternoon I reached South Arm Road. The Isuzu awaited. I hopped in and drove toward Andover. I soon encountered the three hikers I had driven to Rangeley.

They had gone to Andover that day and were returning to the trail. I turned around and gave them a ride to the trail, about a mile away, and warned them about the land slide. I then drove back to Andover. The Pine Ellis Hiker Hostel was full, so I stayed at the Andover Road House.

In the morning I saw Crackers and Shady off at the post office. They were being driven to Grafton Notch on ME 26 to hike south, whereas I was to drive south to Gorham, New Hampshire, where US 2 crosses the trail, and from there to hike north.

I got back on the trail and ascended Mount Hayes — then Cascade Mountain. I tented at Trident Col Tentsite. I was all alone that night, and for some reason I was a little bit afraid. I typically tented alone and had been doing so for months, but that night I was spooked for some reason.

Awake at dawn, I discovered I could have slept on a wooden platform, but I had not looked down far enough into the col to find it. I shook off the night and hiked onward. I took my lunch at Gentian Pond Campsite Shelter.

It was windy around the pond but beautiful — so beautiful I didn't want to leave. But leave I did, and finally I reached the New Hampshire–Maine state line, where a young woman hiker was waiting.

The thought crossed my mind that she might have been waiting for me. She had passed me a short time earlier and had asked me about the state line. I told her I was looking for it too and I hoped it would be marked. I offered to take her picture on her cell phone. I took some good shots as she raised her arms triumphantly under the sign welcoming us to Maine. Later we both stayed at the Carlo Col Shelter. I tented out, and she joined some other hikers in the shelter.

In the morning I met Crackers and Shady as I was coming down from the eastern peak of Goose Eye Mountain. They told me that Mahoosuc Notch was not all that hard; they had done it in less than two hours.

Mahoosuc Notch is supposed to be the toughest mile of the entire trail, with boulders and tight squeezes. It is littered with bones of animals that got stranded in the valley below and could not get out. Well, I would see . . .

I then hiked up Goose Eye Mountain's north peak in strong winds. That always made hiking rough going. I reached the west end of Mahoosuc Notch around 2:30 p.m. and pushed on through the one-mile notch and noted the bones of several animals, including a moose. But it was not as hard as I had feared, and I was able to clamber over, under, around and through the boulders. Three times I had to take off my pack and push it through an opening and climb through myself after it or pull it after me. I made it to the east end in two hours and fifteen minutes.

After a rugged day of hiking I was ready to rest. I camped out near a stream that night on the northern side of the notch. A young man named Moss camped next to me. I had seen him at Pine Ellis Lodge several days earlier.

Upon awakening to a new day, I hiked up the Mahoosuc Arm. It was a tough climb and seemed never to end. Nevertheless, by early afternoon I had reached my Buick at Grafton Notch. In the parking lot, four exhausted hikers were resting and snacking. They had passed me earlier and were gathering strength to go on to Baldpate Mountain.

I was at last finished with all of Maine's 280 miles of trail. Southern Maine was the hardest section of the entire trail. The trail went up and down with little attempt to follow contours or grades to make it easier for hikers. However, the Maine section had two advantages over Virginia: no drought and cooler temperatures.

I had been warned by other hikers that New Hampshire was not any easier.

The date was September 1, 2008. I had been in Maine for five and a half weeks. If I had not wasted time hiking to Katahdin twice, I would have spent a half week less. Now it was on to Gorham, New Hampshire for some rest and a zero day.

Lest I forget, a bonus was the fact that I had done sixteen of the 160 miles that awaited me in New Hampshire. These miles had been just as tough as southern Maine, but now they were behind me. I was tired, but I was in love with the hiking. I sensed I had overcome some psychological barriers.

From reading books by other hikers, I had been led to dread the entire tough Maine section, the 100 Mile Wilderness and the infamous Mahoosuc Notch. By completing Maine and the Mahoosuc Notch, I felt that I had survived the worst the trail could throw at me. Also, since I had flip-flopped, I didn't have to worry about meeting an October 15th deadline to reach Baxter Peak on top of Katahdin. I had been able to divide up the 100 Mile Wilderness, thanks to using my vehicles on the Katahdin Ironworks logging roads. What's more, I had hiked over 1,300 miles, with about 900 miles to go.

Without any time limit, I felt that I would be able to complete the trail — if I avoided injury and sickness. In other words, I was feeling my oats and smiling as I rested in the Gorham Motel.

I studied the New Hampshire AT maps and made my plans. I had a certain dread of Mount Washington because of stories I'd heard of how hikers had died there from losing their way. I was hopeful that, with the vehicles, I could divide up the hiking to reduce the risk. For the moment I was simply happy to have Maine behind me and was enjoying a day of rest from the trail.

Looking around town I was able to find hikers who needed a lift to the trail, and I drove them there. I was in a generous mood.

I talked with Jane on my cell phone and told her that it seemed like I had overcome a number of physical and psychological hurdles. Jane was doing okay at home. For now, I was free to continue hiking, and I focused on that as best I could.

Chapter 7

New Hampshire and Vermont

September 1, 2008 to October 15, 2008

After arriving at a motel in Gorham, I rested that night and ate a real meal at the motel. Then I took a zero day at a less expensive motel, The Northern Peaks, which was closer to downtown restaurants.

I loved Gorham. The town seemed unpretentious and down to earth. I felt welcomed everywhere.

After studying trail maps, I drove the next morning to Pinkham Notch Visitor Center, where the trail crosses NH 16. I left the Buick in the parking lot and returned to the trail. I made it up to where a commercial gondola carries tourists, and I stopped for lunch. There I met Bone Lady, a friendly young woman — a strong hiker who did not use hiking poles.

After lunch we both returned to the trail, and I watched her climb up a steep hill without any hiking poles. She easily left me behind, while I just shook my head in amazement.

Slow and Steady

Typical camping arrangement. In this case it is behind
Two Pine Shelter in the Shenandoah National Park.

That night I tented on Wildcat Mountain, Peak A. I was all alone
and a little spooked because of how remote it was. I was okay the next
morning and met Crackers and Shady, who had spent the night at
Carter Notch Hut and were ascending Wildcat Mountain. I told them
where the Buick was parked at the visitor center.

The day before I had taken them to the trailhead at US 2, from
which they were to hike south. I also had given them a key to get in the
Buick and retrieve gear and food that I had stowed in the car for them.

I don't remember much about the next day of hiking, except that
I found a reference to Becca in the Rattle River Shelter. I assumed that
the Becca referred to was the Becca I had met repeatedly in northern Tennessee and southwest Virginia. Some woman and Becca had

taken a break at the shelter, according to the note that had been written at an earlier date.

When I made it back to the trailhead on US 2, I found the right back tire of the Isuzu flat. I put on the spare and drove back to the Northern Peaks Motel in Gorham for the night. I took the flat tire to a service place and had them put on a patch over a large nail-hole puncture.

I planned to return to the trail the next day, but Crackers called and told me that it would be raining and windy. After getting to Pinkham Notch, Crackers and Shady had found a ride back to Gorham and were staying at White Birches Camping Park. Due to the weather, we all agreed to zero the next day. They invited me to a barbecue supper that night at the White Birches campground.

At the campground I found Moss again. He willingly ate an extra helping of food that had been made for me. I gladly let him have it; I had eaten too much already.

On that zero day I also took the opportunity to have the Isuzu's brake-light switch installed. The brake light had been malfunctioning since Buena Vista, Virginia, and Tommy had ordered the part in Millinocket. I was finally able to get it installed because there had been no car repair shops until I reached Gorham. I took advantage of that extra day in more ways than one.

In the morning I took Crackers and Shady back to Pinkham Notch, where they returned to the trail to hike south. In the parking lot I exchanged the Isuzu for the Buick and drove the Buick to Mount Washington and hiked north. There were strong winds and overcast, wet skies. I made it to Madison Springs Hut where Shady and Crackers had just arrived. We all were able to do some chores for a stay that night at the hut.

The next morning I left Madison Springs Hut and very soon found myself in scary conditions. After getting up on Mount Madison, a lightning storm struck with strongly blowing winds and rain. I felt dangerously exposed to the lightning and tried to get cover, but the cover consisted of short, conifer-type trees. I found a cove and stayed there for an hour, separated from my pack with my metal stove and tent poles. I did not feel safe retracing my steps to Madison Spring Hut; the route was just as exposed to the lightning as elsewhere.

I tried to wait out the lightning and after getting encouraged by longer and longer intervals between thunder claps, I picked up my pack only to be greeted with a loud clap of thunder. Finally I decided just to go for it and started down a long ridge north of the mountain. The thunder finally eased up, but the blowing winds kept causing rain to sting my face and produce staccato pings on my rain hood. However, my rain jacket did a good job of protecting my body.

After a three-mile, miserable descent, I made it into real cover in the taller trees below, and the wind no longer blew stinging rain drops onto my face. My boots were wet as were my socks and that made descent harder as they rubbed blisters on my toes. I finally made it to Pinkham Notch and crawled into the Isuzu, grateful to be free of the rain, and drove back to Gorham and a motel; a cleansing shower and Chinese food hit the spot. I worried, though, about how Crackers and Shady had fared in the lightning storm.

On the following morning I drove to Crawford Notch where US 302 crosses the trail. I started a beautiful day of hiking in clear, cloudless, cool weather.

On top of Mount Webster I met Flip and Flop, a young married couple, and her (Flop's) father, who, like me, could not keep up with them. The young couple were hardened thru-hikers who had taken their names in Georgia. They had somehow managed to get rides to a number of trailheads and walk south over a number of sections like Tommy and me. They had carried the trail names ever since.

I tried to remember them from the south, and they tried to remember me, but we could not recall earlier meetings.

I made it to Mizpah Spring Hut but camped at the close-by Nauman Tentsite for a modest eight dollar fee. It was cold that night, but my trusty sleeping bag and tent did their jobs. I left a water bottle outside and it froze, but the bottles inside the tent didn't freeze.

The morning after, I hurried to inquire after Crackers and Shady at Mizpah Spring Hut, but they were not there. Meanwhile, the weather was beautiful and somewhat warmer — but still cool on the exposed heights.

I was relieved to be climbing Mount Washington on a clear day.

The trail up Mount Washington — rugged, to say the least — but common throughout Maine and New Hampshire.

This made it less likely that I would get lost in fog. Hikers had died from getting lost on Washington, and I had long worried about the climb.

At the Lakes of the Clouds Hut I met Easy Strider taking a noon break. This young thru-hiker remembered me from down south, and

The author in front of Lake of Clouds Hut in New Hampshire.

his face was familiar to me. Yes, I remembered him from Virginia.

I left the Lakes of the Clouds Hut for Mount Washington peak. Easy Strider soon passed me.

To my great relief I met Crackers and Shady on the summit, where we had an emotional group hug. I had assumed that they had already hiked on south and that I had missed them, but they had stayed at Madison Springs Hut an extra night due to the lightning and blowing rain. They had been worried about my safety in the lightning. They

Author atop Mount Washington on a clear day.
The tourists behind him arrived at the summit by car.

The view from the top of Mount Washington.
Note the piles of rocks used as trail markers.

had even hiked down to a road crossing the day before and had rested in Gorham. They had been taken back to the trail, and, by luck, I was reaching the Mount Washington summit just at the moment they were at the top.

I was happy and surprised to see Crackers and Shady, and they were relieved to learn that I had survived the lightning storm. They had left some gear in the Buick, which was parked in the lot at the base of Mount Washington. We planned to meet again, but it would be complicated because I had no cell phone. I had mailed it home for my daughter's use, but it turned out that she bought a new one and mailed mine back to me. I was later to pick up the cell phone farther south in New Hampshire.

So, we decided to leave notes in the Buick and on the Isuzu to guide us in getting back together. After telling them where I had parked the truck, I wished them luck and entered the visitor center. I enjoyed hot dogs with Easy Strider and Last Minute, another thru-hiker I remembered from Virginia. From them I learned that Scout and Harvest were several days behind. They had last seen Scout and Harvest in Hanover, New Hampshire.

Harvest had to leave the trail from there to attend a wedding, and she was behind. I offered to take Easy Strider and Last Minute into town, but they wanted to hike on from the Mount Washington summit.

I reached to the Buick and drove back to Gorham for my final night there. The next day I took a zero at The Carriage Motel in North Woodstock, New Hampshire. I picked up eye drops, which Jane had sent to the post office, and mailed notarized documents that Jane needed. Then I rested in the motel and dried out my boots.

Back on the trail at Franconia Notch the following morning, I began four days of very tough hiking. The rocky trail, steep ascents

Muddy hiking in New Hampshire.

and steep descents, wind and rains all combined to make the hiking slow. Over the twenty-eight miles from Franconia Notch to Crawford Notch, I averaged seven miles a day.

On the first day I had good weather and great views from both Mount Lincoln and Mount Lafayette. Unfortunately, my boot slipped from under me going up Mount Lafayette and I slid down the side of a boulder. Had I not been caught in the branches of a fir tree, I might've been seriously injured or worse — such as landing far down in the canyon below. But the tree stopped me, held me, and I climbed up onto the rocky trail from which I had slipped.

When I was safe I began to tremble; I had come very close to dying. I pulled myself together and made it over Mount Lafayette. As soon as I hiked down to the tree line, I tented out among the firs.

Over and over throughout the night I thought about my fall and how lucky I was to have been stopped by the tree. My right thigh was sore from the fall — a constant reminder of my survival. It was a restless night at best.

The rocky path I had to follow the next day proved to be five miles of rough hiking. I tented just south of Galehead Hut. Shortly after putting up my tent, Shady and Crackers arrived, hiking south and planning to make it to a campsite farther south. I gave them directions to my Buick, but as it turned out, they missed its location two days later.

I awakened to cool, strong winds in the morning. According to Crackers, seventy-mph gusts were predicted for the day. I climbed South Twin Mountain, and the winds were strong indeed. I considered going back down to Galehead Hut to wait out the weather, but a group of four women hikers came up from the hut and said they were going to Zealand Falls Hut, ten miles north. So, I decided I would keep on going.

The winds blew away my pack cover — and good riddance — it was poor protection against the rain. I meant to get a new cover for over a month, and now I would have to do it. (As it turned out, however, Shady gave me one of her spare pack covers when we met again.)

Trying to ignore the weather, I hiked on over Mount Guyot. On the way up I stopped for lunch and met Rock-man, the British-Indian fellow I had met repeatedly in Virginia. He remembered me, but we didn't remember trail names. I then remembered calling him Rock-man.

He didn't understand why I called him that.

I explained it was because Harvest had told me about that crazy seven-pound rock he carried around. He said he had long ago discarded it!

Rock-man was with another young hiker I'd last seen in Virginia. He had always carried an artificial parrot on his shoulder, and he was carrying it today. What next?

I learned from them that Harvest and Scout were a few days behind them and that the three Canadian women had grown weary of the trail and had dropped off.

I took their pictures, wished them well and off they went.

That night I made it to Zealand Falls Hut and worked for my stay by cleaning off the book shelves under direction of the crew. We had a real supper after the paying customers had finished theirs.

I met Tennessee Jim again. I had passed him earlier going north. I also met Just Jill for the first time. She had flip-flopped up to Main from Harpers Ferry and, like me, was now progressing south.

The next day, along with Tennessee Jim, who over the years had hiked numerous sections of the trail, I hiked back to the Isuzu at Crawford Notch. After we arrived, I drove him to the Highland Center, operated by the Appalachian Mountain Club; he had reserved a room there for the night. Tennessee Jim was in his sixties

At Zealand Falls Hut, Just Jill took a photo of the author with his camera while he was putting mole skin on his blistered toes.

and he was undecided about whether to get off or to proceed for a few more days.

I drove to the Econo Lodge in Lincoln, New Hampshire. From

the room phone I called Crackers on her cell and learned that she and Shady had missed directions to my Buick; but, they had just been picked up from the trail by someone who shuttled hikers.

I told them I was at the motel, and soon they were there and checked into the room next to me. We all agreed that, after the tough section we had completed, we would take a zero day. We needed a rest and some good food.

After two nights and a day of rest, I drove Crackers and Shady to Franconia Notch, from where they would hike south. I swapped the Isuzu for the Buick and drove to Kinsman Notch on NH 112 and started hiking north.

I don't remember where I spent the first night back on the trail or if I met Crackers and Shady. But the day afterward I came to Franconia Notch, where US 3 crosses, and went for the Isuzu in the parking lot. Then I headed for a night in North Woodstock at The Carriage Motel to rest and to eat real food again.

I drove to Glencliff, New Hampshire the next morning at the crossing of the trail by NH 25. I met Crackers and Shady after they had descended Mount Moosilauke. I gave them directions to where I had parked the Isuzu. I warned them about the tricky ford that awaited them just before NH 25. I also told them about the first pastures we would find in New England. From there on southward to Pen Mar Park, Maryland, where I had flipped, there would be few above-tree-line climbs, and the hiking would be easier — at least, according to all the books I'd read about the AT.

We were all ready for a break from the hard climbing, but I still had Mount Moosilauke to do to the north. The mountain was beautiful, and I took a number of pictures. I tented out on the north side of the mountain.

The sign at the summit of Mount Moosilauke.

After a steep, dangerous descent the next morning, I came to my Buick at Kinsman Notch where NH 112 crosses. I remember reading a historical marker there, memorializing a World War II military aircraft that crashed on a training mission.

I drove the Buick to Lyme, New Hampshire, where I spent the night at a bed and breakfast.

In the morning I picked up my cell phone Jane mailed to me. I would use it to keep in touch with Crackers.

A ski lodge close by let me park my vehicle in their parking lot, which was close to where the Lyme-Dorchester Road crosses the trail. From there I started north and was met by an elder hostel group that was also going north. When they learned that I had hiked most of the entire trail and got my trail name, they made a big friendly fuss over what I was doing. I let them go on ahead of me. Nevertheless, I soon afterward passed them on the way up Smarts Mountain.

I don't recall where I tented that night. But on the next day I made it to Ore Hill camp and slept inside the shelter. The following day was strange — no views. As I passed Mount Mist, it was all woods. I had lunch there and rested a bit. By mid-afternoon, I reached the Isuzu at Glencliff on NH 25 and drove to the nearby Hikers Welcome Hostel, where I spent a pleasant night — after a hot shower — for a modest fee. The hostel owners had heard about me from Crackers and others, and when I drove in they knew that Slow and Steady had finally made it.

In The Sandwich Shop at Glencliff, I had real food and met a southbound hiker named Z. He was working at the hostel because he was out of money. I gave him $20 and wished him good luck. And the greatest thrill of all came when I wrote an entry in the hiker log.

I sat down to write in the hikers' log but first reviewed the entries over the past several weeks. I experienced a great thrill to find that Harvest had made an entry on September 14, 2008. I looked over the last several weeks to see if Harvest and Scout had been there, and, sure enough, Harvest had made an entry in the log on September 14. I calculated that she and Scout passed by Franconia Notch when I was taking a zero with Crackers and Shady at the Econo Lodge in North Woodstock. I was concerned that they had a very tall task to make it to Katahdin by October 15. I knew they were faster than I was, but I was still worried. (They did make it on October 15, 2008 and sent photos out to fellow hikers, including me. I received the photos after returning home in December.)

I drove back to Lyme, New Hampshire the next day and stayed again at the bed and breakfast. I studied the trail guide about Hanover and how hard it was to park there because of the college. I decided to park eight miles down into Vermont at West Hartford, where the trail crosses Podunk Road.

In West Hartford, Vermont I discovered Just Jill, Moss and another young male hiker taking time out at the country store. I wished them good luck and suspected that this would be the last time I would see the swift, southbound hikers. (I never did see any of them again.) Moss and friend were planning to hike north on the Long Trail when they arrived at it in a few days. As for me, I finally I got back on the trail at Podunk Road.

I hiked onward to Norwich, Vermont, across the river from Hanover. I was able to make cell phone contact with Crackers, who had a good deal for me. She had a friend who lived on a farm outside of Norwich, and she and Shady were staying with him. The kind host invited me to join them that night. They gave directions to a grocery store, where the host, Shady and Crackers picked me up and drove me out to the farm. I was treated to real food, beer and a shower. I spent the night in a cabin below the main house.

Just Jill taking a rest in front of the Country Store in West Hartford, Vermont.

After such a great night of hospitality, I was taken into Norwich, and I set off on the last eighteen miles of New Hampshire, while Shady and Crackers decided to spend two zeros at the farm.

It was threatening rain as I passed over the river into Hanover. I followed the trail through town and then got up into the hills to the east and started climbing. It began raining and blowing hard. I made it to Moose Mountain Shelter and, to my relief, found that there was plenty of room. Due to the rain I was worried I might not find a spot. Only one other hiker was there, and he had the best spot, one that protected him from the weather. I made a place for myself deep in the shelter and stayed mostly dry and warm.

On the following day I came to my car at the Lyme-Dorchester Road at the Dartmouth Skiway. I then drove to the farm, where I had been kindly invited to spend the night. The host and my hiking buddies were out at a restaurant, but they soon returned, let me shower, and allowed me to sleep in the close-by cabin, where I was by myself.

I was happy to be finished with New Hampshire and the tough White Mountain hiking. The trail had become easier after the Whites, and I was making better mileage with less exhaustion. It was now late September, and I felt the trail would be "downhill" from here on.

How wrong could I be?

Well, it proved never to be easy, no matter where I was!

From the farm, the Buick and I traveled to where Woodstock Stage Road crosses the trail, close to South Pomfret, Vermont. I parked there and got back on the trail and reached the Isuzu twelve miles away in West Hartford. I had intended to get a motel in Norwich and get the blinker system fixed on the truck the next morning, but the hotels were so expensive that I called Crackers, and she obtained permission for me to return to the farm and spend the night. So, for the third time, I spent the night in the cabin, at no cost, as well as enjoying free food and beer. In the morning, Crackers fixed my blinkers. The fuse needed to be pulled out, tweaked and put back in. My blinker troubles were behind me, we said our goodbyes to the host and left the farm for good.

I shuttled Crackers and Shady to West Hartford, and they would hike south. Shady had bought a new guitar and would be trying it out on the trail.

I drove south to where VT 100 crosses the trail, close to Gifford Woods State Park, and I started hiking north, past the expensive but hiker-friendly lodge on Kent Pond. I made it to Stony Brook Shelter and tented out behind it.

Two "old" hikers, in their sixties like me, were already in the shelter, and I found it easier to tent out for privacy. There were animal noises all around me that night. Of course, I had hung my food high up, away from bears, so no worry there.

The next day I climbed up to Lakota Lake Lookout and took a lunch break. A northbound hiker came by. He was in his sixties, as well, and he started asking questions about my hike.

I explained about my vehicles.

Southbound hikers (Just Jill, perhaps?) had told him about me, and he even knew my trail name. He said that the AT hiking community is a linear community, one in which we all came to know one another.

We wished each other good luck, and he hiked on.

Later I met Crackers and Shady as they were taking a break at Wintturi Shelter. The day before they had driven the Buick to the post office in Woodstock, Vermont and mailed home the new guitar that Shady had bought in Hanover. Shady found it too heavy for hiking.

I had now given them the keys to the Buick so they could use it whenever they needed it. I had decided not to extend the privilege for the Isuzu because Tommy had not given permission.

Meanwhile, I described where to get water — just before Stony Brook Shelter, a tricky location. But when you knew where it was, you found it easily enough. They left for the cabin on top of Lakota Lake Lookout and spent the night there, well protected from the rains that came hard that night. I slept in the Wintturi Shelter by myself and enjoyed excellent, dry protection from the rain. Next morning I hiked on and reached my Buick at Woodstock Stage Road.

I drove to Woodstock to pick up a postal package from Jane. I then hurried along in the Buick to the coin laundry. After I'd done my clothes, I couldn't crank up the Buick. I waited an hour and was able to get it started. I set off for another trailhead to the south. But before driving out of Woodstock, the battery went dead. I was fortunate to be able to pull to a stop close to a highway work crew. They were kind enough to give me a ten-minute charge on the Buick's battery, and the car started. I turned around and drove to the closest motel in Woodstock.

I called Tommy, and he said it was the alternator, which wasn't recharging the battery. I spent the night at the motel and sent messages by cell to Crackers about my problem. The next morning I called a Sunoco station that was recommended by the motel owner. They didn't have a tow truck. I took a risk and just cranked up the Buick, which started, and drove without incident to the station. I parked it and asked them to put in a new alternator, if needed.

Promptly they went to work. They could not crank it and did tests that showed that the alternator was indeed the problem. They had to get another alternator from Norwich. So, I checked into a motel across the street from the station and enjoyed an unplanned zero in Woodstock.

I took advantage of real food and rest, and finally got in touch with Crackers and explained what happened. They had a slow-down themselves, finding the trail from the Lakota Lake Lookout cabin harder than expected. Thus, they had spent the night at Stony Brook Shelter and were now at the lodge on Kent Pond.

The morning of October 2, 2008 the new alternator was installed, and the Buick then cranked and ran like a champ. I was ready to go back on the trail.

The Buick purred right along to the trailhead on VT 140, from which point I started hiking north. I passed over a beautiful suspension bridge at Mill River. It was dedicated to Robert Brugmann, who drowned trying to cross it in 1974.

I spent the night at Clarendon Shelter all alone. I was visited by the friendly caretaker who came up to the shelter from a nearby road on a three-wheel ATV. He came every evening on his ATV to check on the shelter and the hikers using it — a really nice gesture.

I met Crackers and Shady the following day and told them about the beautiful suspension bridge ahead of them. I invited them to use the Buick to do errands and motels as needed. I don't remember where I spent the ensuing night.

I arose in the morning for a hike to Cooper Lodge. I rested inside the stone shelter.

Later I came to the junction of the AT and the Long Trail. The AT south of this point in Vermont is also the Long Trail. I made it to the Isuzu on VT 100 and drove to the lodge at Kent Pond for the night. There I met an elderly German couple who were touring Vermont. Both were impressed that I was hiking such long distances.

Before I departed in the morning, I called Crackers on her cell phone. They had spent the night at a motel in Rutland. We met that morning in Wallingford, and they stowed some gear in the Isuzu. They drove the Buick to VT 140 and hiked south while I drove the Isuzu to USFS 10 and hiked north, and we met along the way.

When I reached the Buick I took a motel for the night while they kept on the trail and stayed at a shelter south of USFS 10. The following morning I drove the Buick to VT 30/VT 11, walked north and met Crackers and Shady. They gave me a useful tip about a ski patrol cabin on top of Bromley Mountain. It was an empty cabin at this time of year, and hikers could stay there. I stayed there for a night out of the wind, and I was all by myself — once again. Though predicted rains did not come, the wind was strong all night long.

I got up in the morning ready to get on with the hike. Off I went, reaching the Isuzu at USFS 10 in time to spend the night at the Avalanche Motel.

I next drove to the trailhead at VT 9 and hiked north. I met Crackers and Shady along the way. I remember beautiful views south from Glastenbury Mountain.

It was refreshing to see power lines along the trail. Except when the trail is above tree line, it is usually so deeply forested that coming to power lines is like getting into airy space where the sky has opened up to you. It was at a power line crossing that I was able to look back at Glastenbury Mountain and back south to Mount Greylock for breathtaking views. Unfortunately, I was not carrying my camera. I had carried it most of New Hampshire to get photos of Scout and Harvest and others from the south. But after missing Scout and Harvest, I no longer felt the need to carry the camera.

Where I tented or stayed at shelters for the next two nights escapes me because I was so enthralled by the beauty of my hike. The fall leaves were at their peak. I especially liked the yellows and bright reds, and even when it rained the colors came through to brighten up everything — including me.

After reaching the Buick at VT 11 and VT 30, I drove to a motel in southern Vermont on US 7. That night I studied my maps and decided on a place to hike the following day. In the morning, I drove the Buick to Pattison Road in North Adams, Massachusetts and hiked north.

It was there that a difficult ascent up a boulder field brought me onto a ridge where I passed the Massachusetts/Vermont line and soon afterward met Crackers and Shady. I warned them about the boulder slide as well as a blue blaze bypass, which I would have taken had I known about the boulder field. (White blazes mark the AT. Blue blaze trails depart from the main AT and serve as a bypass of certain obstacles, such as a boulder-strewn rock slide.) I also told them where I had parked the Buick in North Adams.

They planned to use the Buick to drive to a motel in Williamstown, Massachusetts and enjoy a zero. Meanwhile, they shared news of an inexperienced hiker with a dog, and I would meet them the next day.

I tented out that night, and on the following day I hiked on until I reached Congdon Shelter.

At the shelter I met the young, inexperienced hiker who had been mentioned to me. His dog barked at me as I came in. The hiker was drying out his clothes (cotton blue jeans) over a fire. He had tented out the night before close to a beaver pond and had gotten wet.

I put my gear in the shelter and cooked supper.

The young man told me he was a college student on break from school and was hiking with his dog. He was otherwise not inclined to communicate, and we both slept in the shelter that night without saying much. I learned the morning, however, that he was trying to get back to North Adams, Massachusetts, where he had left his car and had started hiking three days ago. As I prepared to leave, I offered to take him to North Adams — if he could hike to VT 9 where the Isuzu was parked. He got out of his sleeping bag and started getting his gear ready for hiking.

He and his dog passed me on the trail, and when I reached VT 9, he and the dog were sitting in the back of the Isuzu. I drove them to North Adams and to the public parking site. He and his dog said their goodbyes, climbed into his car and drove off to school.

Crackers had called me the night before and told me about the motel they had taken in Williamstown, Massachusetts. I drove to the motel and got a room next to theirs. That day we enjoyed just taking time off from hiking. For me it was a *nero* day. By nero, hikers mean some hiking, but part of that hiking day is spent in a motel.

It was October 15, 2008, and I had finished another state — Vermont. All of upper New England had been completed, and over 1,600 miles out of the trail's 2,176 were finished. I loved the hiking and was completely confident that, barring some injury, I would be able to hike the entire Appalachian Trail.

The trail in Vermont was a breath of fresh air compared to the rocky, boulder strewn trail in New Hampshire and Maine. I could actually enjoy taking in the views and fall leaves without having to focus on the rocky trail bed itself, like in New Hampshire.

The Dartmouth Outing Club and the Green Mountain Club had done an excellent job on trail maintenance. I considered the Vermont section by far the most enjoyable of the 1,600 miles I had done. I felt that I was probably slowing Crackers and Shady down, but they did not complain and wanted to continue having access to the vehicles.

Chapter 8

Onward to Mid-Pennsylvania

October 16, 2008 to December 6, 2008

In Massachusetts I was finally persuaded by Crackers to do some slack packing. *Slacking* refers to light-weight backpacking, usually for one day, during which one doesn't carry a tent and stove. We chose a thirteen-mile section from Outlook Avenue in Adams, Massachusetts, where we left the Isuzu, to Pattison Road in North Adams, Massachusetts, where we would return to the Buick.

I was amazed by how fast we went. We hiked up Mount Greylock and they took photos of each other and the monument on top. They arrived at the Buick before me, but I made it ten minutes later. We then drove down to Dalton, Massachusetts and spent the night at the Shamrock Motel.

We slacked north again from Dalton to the Isuzu on Outlook Avenue in Adams. The day was beautiful and the fall leaves were breathtaking with autumn colors. Shady took digital photos, some of which she later printed out for me.

The motel in Dalton had given me permission to leave the Isuzu in their parking lot for several nights while I hiked back from the south. Crackers and Shady then started south on the trail at Dalton. I drove the Buick to where MA 23 crosses the trail east of Great Barrington. I then hiked north with a full pack.

I don't remember where I pitched my tent the first night. I tented the next night, though, just north of the side trail to Upper Goose Pond Cabin. It was cold that night, but I was warm inside my trusty tent and sleeping bag.

The next morning I met Crackers and Shady and told them where the Buick was. They actually had cookies and a chicken biscuit from McDonald's for me. Somehow they had found a ride into one of the nearby towns and had remembered how I loved chicken biscuits. How kind!

Once again, I don't remember where I tented that night. But on the following day I made it back to Dalton, Massachusetts. I decided to spend the night at the Shamrock and enjoy real food. I called Crackers and learned that they were staying at the Mountain View Motel on MA 23 in Great Barrington. After a full breakfast in Dalton, I drove to the Mountain View Motel and checked in next to Crackers and Shady. We used the motel as a base of operations for slack-pack hikes for the next two days.

The first was a nine-mile hike from US 7 to MA 23. We took both cars to the MA 23 trailhead and left the Isuzu. They started south. I then traveled with the Buick to the parking lot at a green nursery on US 7, close to the trail crossing. I started north with a light pack and soon met Crackers and Shady. They were flying, and so was I, with our light packs.

After only four hours I had done the nine miles back to the Isuzu and rejoined them at the Mountain View Motel. I had discovered a tear in my right boot, one of the new boots I had bought in Rangeley, Maine. It was too soon for such a failure, so I called the company and they agreed to send me a new replacement pair to be picked up in Pawling, New York.

We decided to do another slack day. They started at US 7 while I started at Jug End Road. We did it in three hours. We met somewhere in the middle, and they warned me about slippery boardwalks through some marshes, but I had no problems there. I came to the historical marker for Shays' Rebellion — finally to arrive at US 7, where I picked up the Isuzu.

While driving back to the motel, a driver blew a car's horn at me at a stop light in Great Barrington. It was Shady, driving the Buick and giving me a friendly greeting. They were going to the library to do e-mail. I returned to the motel and enjoyed my last night there. I was amazed at how fast we did the slack-pack hiking.

Next up was Connecticut.

The next morning we drove to Jug End Road and parked the Isuzu. They started south, and I drove the Buick to Falls Village, Connecticut and parked it in the public lot above the power plant. I hiked to the Iron Bridge, where the highway department had posted signs. Southbound hikers were instructed to take a detour involving roads that added extra miles around a bridge repair site on US 7. The detour was very unpopular with hikers. I proceeded northward and tented out in Salisbury, Connecticut in woods closed in on both sides by houses.

The day afterward I hiked up to Bear Mountain, the highest point in Connecticut. I met Crackers and Shady, and I explained where I had left the Buick. I added with determination, "We must figure out how to avoid that detour."

They promised to think on it.

That night I pitched my tent on Race Mountain in Massachusetts, with reduced visibility and wind. Not so bad, though; I found a cove that sheltered me from the wind. It was a gloomy night, and the next day continued to be cloudy and foggy. I passed through a state park and reached the Isuzu on Jug End Road. I climbed into the truck and off I went to the Mountain View Motel in Great Barrington to spend one last night.

My hiking colleagues spent the night in a motel close to Kent, Connecticut. We talked on our cell phones and arranged to meet at the parking lot above the power plant in Falls Village the next morning. They laughed and claimed to know how to beat the detour we would soon encounter.

Upon arrival at the power plant, Crackers described their plan. We would all drive in the Isuzu to a school parking lot located just north of the site on US 7, where the bridge construction had created the need for hikers to bypass Falls Village. Then we would all slackpack back to the Buick at the power plant — about two miles. Next we would drive the Buick back to the Isuzu and drive both vehicles over the bridge under construction on US 7. Cars and trucks were allowed to pass over the bridge — but not hikers. The road shoulders were blocked by construction equipment, and hikers had no room to walk unless they got onto the road, which was dangerous. We outwitted the detour brilliantly.

After the bridge maneuver we left the Isuzu in a parking lot on the south side of the bridge, and Crackers and Shady hiked south. I drove the Buick to Kent, Connecticut, where CT 341 crossed the trail. From the parking site, I started north. I soon caught up with The Carolina Boys, one in his forties and the other in his fifties, who were doing a section through Connecticut. We made it along River Road and stayed at Stewart Hollow Brook Lean-to.

On the day afterward I met Crackers and Shady. I told them where to pick up the Buick and warned them about difficult hiking around John's Ledges. Later The Carolina Boys and I spent the night in the Pine Swamp Brook Lean-to. It was the last night that I had company in an AT shelter. The population of hikers had decreased significantly because of the increasingly cool season.

That night, heavy rains started at 3:00 a.m., but it felt snug inside. We had to leave the next morning. The older and slower Carolina Boy left at 6:00 a.m. in heavy rain. I left at 8:00 a.m., as did the other Carolina Boy. By then the rain was lighter but persistent.

We caught up with the slow one just before the US 7 bridge. I was able to take them both across the bridge-under-construction in the Isuzu, thereby saving them from a three-mile detour in the rain. They proceeded north along the traditional trail.

I drove back to CT 341, following a hunch that I might see my hiking colleagues, Crackers and Shady. Sure enough, they were just hiking up to the Buick. The rains that morning had delayed their start. We drove together to a restaurant in Kent and had lunch.

We crossed into New York and took rooms at the Duchess Motor Lodge in Wingdale. The next day Crackers and I drove first to Bull's Bridge in Connecticut to leave the Isuzu, then she took me to CT 341, close to Kent, Connecticut and dropped me off for a southbound slack hike.

I hiked into New York and back into Connecticut in cold, windy conditions and reached the Isuzu at Bull's Bridge. I drove to Pawling, New York and picked up the replacement boots at the post office. Finally, I returned to the Duchess Motor Lodge in Wingdale for a second night.

The next morning we all climbed into the Buick, and I drove Crackers and Shady to CT 341 where they started south. I drove the Buick to where NY 52 crosses the trail and started north. I purchased two hot dogs at a convenience store where NY 55 crosses the trail. I went past Nuclear Lake and made it to Telephone Pioneers Shelter, only to spend a cold night by myself. The day following I met Crackers and Shady at Old Route 22.

I had taken off my shirt, eaten some lunch and was basking in the sun when they came along. I told them where the Buick was parked. That meeting would be the last for six days, since I was planning to go back to Virginia to vote in the November 4 presidential election.

"Look, you can use the Buick any way you want as long as, on the sixth day, you leave it at New York fifty-two for my return. And don't slow your hiking for me. If you want to go south without me, I understand. It's okay, I won't be offended."

They were officially noncommittal, but it seemed they preferred staying with the car. When I departed I did not know if I would see them again and wished them the best.

Soon after I met Crazy Feet and Hobbit. Crazy Feet was a thirteen-year-old girl, and Hobbit was her mother. Just Jill had alerted me to the duo back in Vermont and thought they were only a few days behind her. So, I had finally met them. I did not try to talk to them because they seemed intent on moving on. Later they were to be with Crackers and Shady at The Mayor's House in Unionville, New York.

(Hobbit and Crazy Feet had their pictures taken at the ATC Headquarters in Harpers Ferry, West Virginia. The occasion was the moment of completion of their 2008 thru-hike. They had flip-flopped at Harpers Ferry, as had Just Jill, but at slightly different times. Their picture appears on page 26 of the May–June 2009 edition of *Journeys*, the ATC magazine that, in that edition, listed names of all those who completed thru-hikes for 2008.)

At some point, after meeting Hobbit and Crazy Feet, I blundered off the main trail and onto an old, abandoned section that still had blazes, which in some places had worn out and in other places were still visible. After ninety minutes of frustration and uncertainty about whether I was on the right trail, I backtracked and finally stumbled onto the modern, well-blazed trail. Later I spent the night at Wiley Shelter — another cold night by myself.

I reached Bull's Bridge in Connecticut the next day and drove the Isuzu to Hartford, Connecticut, where I checked into a motel. The next day, November 2, I flew home to Norfolk, Virginia so I could vote in the November 4th presidential election. I also completed some dental work, thanks to my wife having made arrangements with the dentist.

I was pleased with the Obama win and with the Democratic advances throughout the country on November 4. I also enjoyed resting off the trail. It was good to be home for a few days with Jane and my children, Karen and Jonathan.

Karen's boyfriend was in Switzerland, working as a computer specialist, and she missed him. She was also waiting for results of several job applications that she had submitted for work in her field of wildlife conservation. So, she was in a state of uncertainty in two directions.

Jonathan was in a state of denial about an illness and about the need to take medication for it. But he was looking for a job, and he wanted to buy a used car to make it possible to work. I went with him to the auto salesman and helped with half of the payment.

I returned to finish the trail and arrived back at Hartford on November 7. I got into the Isuzu, which I had parked at the airport, and drove to meet Crackers and Shady where I had left the Buick on NY 52.

They had done some hiking while I was gone but had not wanted to go far ahead and lose contact with me and the vehicles. We left the Isuzu at NY 52 and drove the Buick to a motel close to Bear Mountain State Park. They had already done the section between that park and NY 52.

The next day they took me to Bear Mountain State Park. We left the Buick there, and they started south while I started north. That day I crossed the Hudson River on the Bear Mountain Bridge. At 200 feet above sea level, it is one of the lowest points on the Appalachian Trail. Actually, the lowest point seems to be the Trailsides Museum & Zoo in the state park, officially 124 feet above sea level.

On the east side of the Hudson, I looked up into the hills, above which I would climb to get up out of the valley. I was back on the trail again, and it felt good.

I probably tented out on Denning Hill the first night. I remember that just before stopping to put up my tent my wife called me on my cell and heard my winded answers to her questions. To her, I sounded out of breath and she hoped that the trail was not too much for me. I assured her that I was well and that I usually called her when I was resting — not while climbing hills.

I slept well that night and was off again the next morning to the long ridge of Shenandoah Mountain where I set up my tent under an evergreen tree for the night. Rains and wind came, but I was comfortable. The next day I stopped at the RPH Shelter for lunch and used a rusty water pump to refill my water bottles. I reviewed the shelter log to see if any old friends had been there but did not find anything.

The trail passed over a series of roads that I crossed on foot, including the Taconic State Parkway, which appeared to be made with concrete from the 1950s. Later I came to the Isuzu on NY 52.

I called Crackers, who had checked in at "The Mayor's House" in Unionville, New York. "The Mayor" was the actual mayor of Unionville, and trail hikers were welcome to stay at his house. The Mayor was a kind, seventy-year-old man who opened his house for hikers, partly in memory of his late wife who had been a hiker friend for years.

To the hiking community, their home was affectionately called The Mayor's House. I received an invitation from the Mayor and directions from Butch, one of the Mayor's helpers. After a number of false turns I finally arrived in Unionville, New York after dark.

Butch was waiting for me at a road junction, and I followed his car to The Mayor's House. I was welcomed by the Mayor, Butch, Bill (an eighty-year-old man who seemed to be staying with the Mayor), and Shady and Crackers. I must not forget to mention a British man who was also staying at The Mayor's House, but I forget his trail name; he came every year to hike sections of the trail.

Crackers showed me where Harvest and Scout had put in an entry weeks earlier. I looked at their pictures and confirmed that it was indeed them. I slept in a bunk in the basement of The Mayor's House. I took a shower upstairs opposite The Mayor's bedroom. I was treated to breakfast the next morning by the eighty-year-old cook, Bill.

There was no official charge for these services, but hikers were allowed to give what they could afford. A large donation jar was on prominent display in the kitchen.

I left a one hundred dollar check at the end of my stay — five nights in all. Twenty dollars a night for a bunk, breakfast and shower, as well as shuttling services, is a deal made in heaven.

The Mayor thought the donation was very generous.

I laughed and said, "I think that's a good deal."

He responded by saying, "I like a win-win situation!"

The next morning I followed The Mayor and parked the Isuzu where NY 17A crosses the trail. I was northbound to Bear Mountain. The first night I tented just north of the Orange Turnpike and lost my headlamp. It may have been lost in the vigor of suspending my food bag. I looked and looked but could not find it. I left it behind, wherever it was.

The next night I slept at William Brien Memorial Shelter by myself. It was cold and the moon was out — just a little spooky. During the night I could see deer walking around outside. The next day did come, and I made it to Bear Mountain where I met Footnote at the summit.

I was not interested in going up to the observation tower, but he was. This southbound hiker in his sixties had stories to tell about how he had been snowed in at Mount Greylock in Massachusetts. He told me that Alaska and Shepherd were a few days behind with their dogs. It was a welcome confirmation that they were still on the trail. I had seen Alaska south of the West Branch of the Piscataquis River in Maine. I last heard of them when Crackers remembered seeing them at Grafton Notch on ME 26.

I reached the Buick at the Bear Mountain Visitor Center, and I returned to The Mayor's House in Unionville.

Over the next three days I took three slack hikes: nine miles, seventeen miles and nine miles, mostly on the New Jersey side of the New York/New Jersey line. Some of the easiest hiking on the entire trail occurred on those days. Maybe it was easy because I carried a light pack, or maybe it was related to the flatness of much of the trail from NY 17A to High Point State Park headquarters on NJ 23.

Anyway, it began with Crackers dropping me off in the rain at Warwick Turnpike, and I hiked north to the Isuzu on NY 17A. The next day she dropped me at the Warwick Turnpike, and I hiked south seventeen miles to Unionville, New York in cloudy weather.

I drove the next day with Crackers and Shady to High Point State Park, then I hiked north to Unionville, spending the last of five nights at The Mayor's House. Shady and Crackers felt that they had been in the kind Mayor's House long enough and spent a night in a motel in New Jersey.

The stay at The Mayor's House was one of the high points for me during the entire hike. The Mayor told me, "I have no intention of hiking myself, but I admire hikers and their subculture."

The Mayor had taken in eighty-year-old Bill, who lived at the house and cooked breakfast for hikers and the Mayor. Helper Butch was in his forties and was a frequent visitor at The Mayor's House. He shuttled hikers to and from the trail and helped them with the internet at the house.

(Since my hike, the Mayor retired and now lives in a different town.)

At the end of my stay I said goodbye to all three Trail Angels, and I drove the Isuzu to High Point State Park headquarters, where I met Crackers and Shady with the Buick.

I was to hike south from there, while they drove both vehicles to different locations south, leaving one at US 206 at Culvers Gap. They were to stay at Forest Motel, close to Branchville, New Jersey with the other vehicle. I reached Culvers Gap at the end of the day and drove to the Forest Motel, where I took a room next to them.

At last I was back even with them in miles hiked since I left for the November 4 election. I had hiked every day since returning from the vote, and they had taken a couple of zeros. I knew I had slowed them down and felt bad about it, but they had chosen to slow down and to stick with me and the cars.

The next two days were slack-pack hikes, with me hiking south and them hiking north for a change. I started at US 206 and went south on a cold, windy and cloudless day. On the ridge of Rattlesnake Mountain I came across three men who were viewing raptors with binoculars. I don't know if they were professional wildlife workers or just amateur raptor enthusiasts, but they were out in the cold and wrapped up tight against the icy wind.

I later met Crackers and Shady, and we discussed where we had parked the vehicles. We moved on, and I reached the Buick, where CR 602 crossed the trail, and drove back to the Forest Motel for my second night. They drove to the motel after they reached Culvers Gap.

The day afterward I left the Isuzu at Millbrook-Blairstown Road/ CR 602 and hiked south again. Shady and Crackers had parked the Buick at the Headquarters of Delaware Water Gap National Recreation Area (DWGNRA) and hiked north. We met somewhere in the middle.

A rocky trail made it hard to get around Sunfish Pond, but I managed to get to the Buick at the DWGNRA. As I was about to drive off, Shady drove in with the Isuzu. We mapped out strategy, and, with help from a Pennsylvania tourist office, we found a motel in nearby Stroudsburg. We spent the night there, and bright and early in the morning I drove to Delaware Water Gap headquarters and hiked south, while they drove to Fox Gap on PA 191 and hiked north. When we met along the trail, we exchanged info on where the cars were parked and walked on briskly. It was cold, really cold. I reached PA 191 and drove back to the motel for a second night.

On November 19, 2008 Crackers and Shady told me that, due to the cold weather, it was no longer fun for them; they were going home.

I was sad, of course, but I completely understood and supported them in their tough decision. I had only 200 miles to go before finishing the entire trail. I couldn't think of stopping now, even with the sometimes-bitter cold.

I decided to stay an extra night at the motel, which would allow them to use my room while I hiked another section during the day. They were to catch the bus that evening, so, I drove to Wind Gap, Pennsylvania, where PA 33 crosses the trail, and started north. I made quick time, but at Wolf Rocks I nearly had a bad fall from stumbling over a boulder. Once again I saved myself by grabbing onto a tree.

I made it to PA 191, called Crackers, and, while I was waiting for Crackers to pick me up, I met a charming young woman who was going north. She was hoping to get to Delaware Gap and the Church Hostel. I told her not to miss The Mayor's House in Unionville, New York. She did not want a ride when Crackers drove up with the Buick. We wished her good luck and drove back to the motel. I later took Crackers and Shady to the bus station in Delaware Water Gap, Pennsylvania, and they caught a bus back to Tennessee.

The day afterward they called me, announcing their safe arrival at their home in Tennessee. I had enjoyed being with them for over three months, but I knew they could have been farther south had they not slowed down to stay with the vehicles. In all, they had done 1,500 miles of the trail.

That same morning I drove the Buick to Little Gap where Blue Mountain Road crosses. It was cold and windy. I spent the night at Leroy A. Smith Shelter, for the first time using Tommy's large sleeping bag. His bag insulates you down to fifteen degrees, and it is heavier than my thirty degree sleeping bag. But I was warm inside, and that's what counted. I left one of my water bottles outside my bag, and it froze solid, but a bottle kept inside the bag did not freeze.

My fingers grew numb from the cold the next morning when I had to put my sleeping bag and other gear in my backpack. I pushed on, though, and came to Wind Gap. Much to my relief, the Isuzu cranked right up, even in dead cold. I went to the Travel Motel in Wind Gap, Pennsylvania for the afternoon and the remainder of the cold day and even colder night.

In the morning I drove to Lehigh Gap where PA 873 crosses and climbed up onto a ridge that overlooked the town of Palmerton, Pennsylvania. I was surprised to see hunters stalking along in blaze orange. Ah, I thought, hunting season has started. In time I encountered numbers of hunters through the rest of Pennsylvania.

I reached the Buick at Little Gap and drove to Slatington, Pennsylvania. I found a room at Fine Lodging, where I spent two days. A fellow named Ira Fine ran the place and offered rooms for reasonable rates. I don't remember why I spent the second night there. However, the cold weather and predicted rains were probably what caused me to take a zero. I enjoyed just hanging around, reading and resting and eating real food.

After the zero I drove back to Little Gap and swapped out the Buick for the Isuzu, drove to Port Clinton, Pennsylvania and parked at the PA 61 trailhead. Over the next three days I hiked north.

The first night I met a lovely family day-hiking in the vicinity of Pulpit Rock. It was late in the afternoon, and it seemed to me that they were in danger of being stranded out after dark without camping gear. I showed them my map, and to my relief they thought it best not to go off on a doubtful trail to the west. They decided to retrace their steps down to a parking lot from which they had started earlier in the afternoon.

Later I tented out on a ridge, and it was warm enough — as long as I was inside the tent with wool gloves and wool socks on. But when I had to take down the tent the next morning, it was too cold. My fingers were especially cold, and I could not keep in my wool gloves. I needed fine finger coordination to untie the food bag from up in the trees, undoing the tent pegs and poles, and for stuffing the tent into its sack. My fingers remained numb until the gloves and hiking warmed them up.

The days were now so short that I had only eight hours of hiking, at the most. I had reduced my food to jerky, cheese, GORP and chocolate bars; therefore, I didn't need a stove to cook freeze-dried meals. My pack was bulky, not due to weight but due to extra woolens and wraps I used for the cold nights in the tent. The cold nights also made shorter hikes more desirable, and the frequent road crossings in Pennsylvania made it possible to break the hike into shorter sections. The current section required three nights in tent or shelter, longer than most of my sections in Pennsylvania. After an eight-hour hike on the second day, I pitched my tent close to Tri-County Corner.

The morning after was still cold. I stopped at a shelter (probably Allentown Hiking Club Shelter) and called Jane on my cell. Another hiker, southbound, stopped at the shelter just as I was finishing with Jane. We started talking, and he identified himself as Warren Doyle. I recognized the name immediately from books and from seeing a videotape documentary about the trail community. He is a legendary hiker and AT advocate who has done the entire AT seven times. He was, he said, out again — this time for the spiritual aspect of hiking. He was surprised to see a thru-hiker so late in the season.

I took his picture, then set off again north. (I carried my camera to get in some photos of the last weeks of the trail.)

I stayed at the Bake Oven Knob Shelter that night, another cold one. Finally, on the day after, I reached the Buick at Lehigh Gap and drove to Port Clinton and checked on the Isuzu. It was unmolested and obviously had not been towed. I had been a little worried about whether it was parked legally, but everything was fine.

I checked in to the Port Clinton Hotel for the night, then I walked back to retrieve the Isuzu and park it in a public lot down across the river below the hotel.

After a night in a warm room, I said goodbye to the Buick in the public lot and drove the Isuzu down to PA 501 and started north. I don't remember where I tented out, but it was cold. In the morning I had to push the snow from the tent because its weight sagged down its sides. I got my gear stowed, the tent back in its bag and pushed on to Port Clinton.

Once again, snow removal from the Buick's windshield was necessary. Once it was cleared I drove to Pine Grove, Pennsylvania, where I checked into a room at the Colony Lodge for two nights. I was planning to do two days of slack packing.

The Colony Lodge was managed by South Asian Indians, as was the case for a number of motels I stayed at throughout the hike. I asked one Indian motel owner why there were so many Indian managers. He said the job offered a way for the parents to work at "home" and have their children at "home" each night. His Indian family with children lived in the office apartment, similar to so many other Indian managed motels.

The first morning I drove to the point where the trail and PA 72 go through Swatara Gap, and I parked the Buick. I hiked north and stopped for a break at the William Penn Shelter. Then I went on to PA 501 and drove the Isuzu back to Colony Lodge. There I spent the next two nights while slack hiking. Except for a couple of times with Crackers and Shady, I always carried a tent in case I was injured and could not make it back to the trailhead. So, in one sense, my slack hikes were not always completely slack hikes.

It was very cold the second day, and I was happy when the truck cranked right up. I then drove to PA 225 where the footbridge takes hikers over what used to be a dangerous road crossing.

I started north and tented out on the ridge of Stony Mountain. That night I heard deep panting sounds of some animal that had climbed up to the ridge from below. The panting, of course, made me think bear, but it was probably a deer; whatever the animal was, it had deep lungs and knew how to use its lungs to recover from steep climbing. The animal, for all I knew, had just escaped with its life; I was reminded of the hunters I had recently seen. The panting soon stopped, and I slept well.

The following night I slept at Rausch Gap Shelter, which offered a good, piped spring flowing into a bird bath-like structure. There I read the hikers' log, and Just Jill had put in a note referring to me, Shady, Crackers, Crazy Feet, Hobbit and Moss. She had been there two weeks earlier and wished all of us good luck.

In the morning I made it back to the Buick at Swatara Gap. I then drove to Duncannon, Pennsylvania, and I checked into the Doyle Hotel for two nights. The Doyle Hotel is about one hundred feet off the trail, which goes through Duncannon. It is a true hiker haven and a convenient way to get off the trail for a night or two, depending on space available. At that time of year, I was the only hiker registered.

Several weeks earlier Just Jill had called me from the Doyle, wishing me well. Hobbit and Crazy Feet must have gone through a week

The Doyle Hotel in Duncannon, Pennsylvania, a hiker's heaven.

or so earlier. My room was an old fashioned one with a steam heater. My window overlooked the street. The dimensions of the room were small, but I had plenty of room to put down my pack and lie comfortably on the bed. There was no TV on which to watch The Weather Channel, but with shorter hikes I did not need weather information as much. There were two common bathrooms and two showers. I was on the second floor, the balcony of which went around and descended outside to the parking lot behind the hotel. It was luxury, at least by hiker standards.

I took advantage of being in civilization and had a real meal at the bar and drank beer. The husband-and-wife owners were kind, unpretentious people who liked hikers and went out of their way to accommodate them.

In the morning I ate a real breakfast across the street at Goodie's Restaurant. I then hiked through town and over the bridge of the Susquehanna River and up the mountain to the north. Looking back from the mountain, I took in a slow panorama of the river and the town of Duncannon below.

Since I had encountered a number of hunters, I displayed my own blaze-orange pieces, and my chartreuse cycling jersey was strapped over my pack and tied to my jacket to make me look different from a game animal.

I took a rest at Clarks Ferry Shelter and left a note to Alaska, Shepherd and Moss, wishing them well. I then hiked on to the Isuzu at PA 225, drove back to Duncannon and ate a late lunch at the All American Truck Plaza. The waitress looked me over and gave me the lunch free; I must have looked like a tramp, the way many hikers do. I left her a generous tip and went back to the Doyle Hotel.

The kind hotel owners, true Trail Angels that they were, readily gave me permission to leave the Isuzu in the hotel parking lot for a week while I drove the Buick up to Lennox, Massachusetts for a yoga and meditation conference at the Kripalu Center with my wife. I left an Isuzu key with them and forgot to get it when I returned; but, I had a backup key anyway, so I didn't think much about it. Several weeks later, back home in Virginia, I received the key in the mail from the Doyle owners.

I had only seventy-four miles to go to complete the trail. Despite missing them, I found that with Shady and Crackers now gone I had more freedom to take a week off for yoga and meditation with Jane. I left the next day for the six-day retreat.

Chapter 9

The Grand Finale

December 7, 2008 to December 23, 2008

It was on December 7, 2008 when I drove up to Lennox, Massachusetts and joined Jane at the Kripalu Center for the meditation retreat. In the doing, I passed by a number of AT sites I had been through only weeks earlier — such as the trail crossings on US 7 where the bridge was being constructed in Connecticut and below Great Barrington, Massachusetts. Though it was snowing on that afternoon, I made it safely to Kripalu in Lennox.

For six days we were treated to the gentle wisdom of Jack Kornfield and his assistants, as well as excellent vegetarian food. I was taught a new kind of walking meditation, very different from hiking the trail, where you have to pay attention to your every step to avoid every injury. This new kind of walking assists one in enhancing the meditative experience.

Six days later, December 13, I saw Jane off as she took the shuttle back to the Albany airport. I then drove back to Pennsylvania to finish the trail, and I stopped again at Colony Lodge in Pine Grove, the very reasonable motel I had used earlier and managed by the South Asian Indians.

After a good night's rest, I drove to the I-81 overpass, where the trail goes over the interstate east of Carlisle, Pennsylvania. I hiked north through farm fields, along streams and over road bridges. I went past the ATC Scott Farm Trail Work Center and then finally up into the woods. I tented out that night next to a stream, well past the Darlington Shelter.

On the next morning I hiked back to Duncannon. It was a clear day, and, as I passed through the town, I happened to look at my re-

flection in a store window. What a sight!

I looked like a tramp with yellow rain gear covering my thermal layers of clothing. Scraps of blaze orange covered my back-pack. I wore a bright orange synthetic head piece — all to alert hunters not to shoot at me.

Finally, I again reached the Doyle Hotel and spent my last night there with the friendly hosts.

From there I drove the Isuzu to where the Buick was parked, close to the I-81 overpass, and swapped vehicles. I drove the Buick to where Hunter's Run Road/PA 34 crosses the trail and started north. I probably spent the night at Alec Kennedy Shelter or tented out close by.

The day after I hiked on — up over Center Point Knob and later down into Boiling Springs, Pennsylvania, where the ATC has its

Mid-Atlantic Office. I stopped briefly to chat with the staff and hurried on. It was raining intermittently, and I needed to get back to I-81. By the end of the afternoon I was back at the I-81 overpass and in the Isuzu driving to Mount Holly Springs, Pennsylvania, where I stayed at the Holly Inn and Restaurant.

The following morning I drove the Buick, after swapping it with the Isuzu, to Pine Grove Furnace State Park and was allowed to park in a lot for several days. I hiked north and soon came to the Midpoint Marker and took pictures. Later I came to the Isuzu at Hunter's Run Road and went back to the Holly Inn for the night.

I next shuttled the Isuzu to Caledonia State Park where US 30 passes. As I parked and got out of the truck, a fellow named Robert Freeman came up to me and wished me good hiking. He talked about how he was a volunteer for the AT and how, dur-

The AT Midpoint Marker with my hiking poles and backpack — 1,069 miles to finish in both directions.

ing the summer, he had done trail maintenance down in Virginia. As he spoke, something rang a bell. It turned out that he and I had met in northern Virginia back in July, the day we sat down on the resting bench close to the Sky Meadows State Park trail. He had been working on trail maintenance that same day and had rested at the same time I did. Having recalled our previous time together, we wished each other well, and I started north.

Snow!

Note the trail blazes and arrow pointing the way — and my backpack.

In Pennsylvania the trail was cold but beautiful
to see, with snow and ice in places.

Tumbling Run Shelters, my last night on the trail.

I spent the night at Birch Run Shelters. It snowed that night, and it was bright the whole night from the snow. To my relief it did not snow deeply. I had feared it getting too deep and losing my way from the white blazes being covered. The next day I passed the two Toms Run Shelters and reached the Buick at Pine Grove Furnace State Park. I had to clear off the snow from my windshield before driving down to Waynesboro, Pennsylvania. There I took a room at a motel, also managed by an Indian family, and ate pizza that night.

From Waynesboro I drove to the county park in Pen Mar, Maryland. I left the Buick at the park and started north. I spent the night at Tumbling Run Shelters.

It was my last night on the trail.

It was cold, and I was alone. In fact, I had slept in the shelters alone since I spent two nights with the Carolina Boys in Connecticut. The day after, I made it to the Isuzu in Caledonia State Park and drove back to the motel in Waynesboro, Pennsylvania.

I called Crackers and Shady, and Jane to give all of them the good news of my completing the trail at last, nine months after starting in Georgia. It was December 21, 2008.

But there was still one special mile to go, I reminded myself. It was the mile up Springer Mountain where I left off back in March, when Tommy and I had done our first three-day hike down from Woody Gap to Springer. It had been hanging over me ever since. So, I would now do it as part of my plan to return the Isuzu to my nephew Gus, who lives in LaGrange, Georgia, close to Tommy.

I also wanted to see Crackers and Shady again. They had invited me to visit them on the way down.

Crackers and Shady with the Isuzu.

On December 22, 2008 I drove down I-81 into Tennessee and that night called Crackers to get directions to their house, close to Ducktown. Early in the afternoon of December 23, 2008 I met Crackers at a rural convenience store and followed her to her house, where Shady greeted us. We took pictures and had group hugs; in fact, some neighbor friends came by and took our pictures — all three of us together — and made a fine fuss over us.

Shady and Crackers in front of their home in Tennessee.

Crackers, the author and Shady on December 23, 2008.

The author, saying goodbye to Shady and Crackers, and on to the last mile.

Since I had to make it to Springer, I said goodbye to my hiker friends and drove up USFS 42 to the trailhead parking lot, one mile north of the Springer Mountain summit.

As was typical of hiking in December, the days were short. It was close to dusk when I arrived at the trailhead. I hiked on up to Springer — the first mile for most — but, for me, the last mile. The trail was slick and icy, and I took care not to injure myself. I finally made it and took pictures of the southern terminus and the first few white blazes. Then I descended back to the Isuzu.

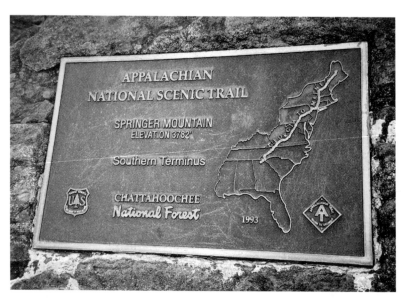

The AT Southern Terminus plaque at Springer Mountain, Georgia.

An interesting, twisted tree at Springer Mountain.

I called Crackers to announce my safe completion of the final mile, then I drove to LaGrange. I arrived late at night and put myself down in George's house, my other brother, who also lives in LaGrange and who, despite being urged by me, never had any intention of hiking the trail. For the next several days I stayed with George and got involved in holiday parties with his friends. I even called Just Jill in Oregon to let her know that I had finished the trail. As usual, she was thrilled, and we wished each other good luck.

Tommy and Gus were out of town at the time. I left the Isuzu at Gus's house, and George took me to the Greyhound Bus stop. I traveled by bus to Atlanta, then to Richmond, then to Washington and, finally, to Hagerstown, Maryland.

At Hagerstown I hired a taxi to take me to Pen Mar Park in Maryland, where I came back to the Buick that had gone undisturbed for the week it sat in the parking lot. I got in and cranked it up without any problem and drove back to my home in Chesapeake, Virginia.

Upon arrival, Jane gave me a recent letter from dear little Scout, the young Virginia Tech graduate who, with Harvest, I had seen repeatedly before I flip-flopped up to Maine. She announced that they had completed the trail on the very last day allowed, October 15, 2008, and enclosed a photo showing them on top of Katahdin. She wanted to know if had I completed the trail. It was dated December 21, 2008, the day I had completed all but the final mile.

I wrote to Scout, telling her how glad I was to hear from her and how we probably missed each other while I was taking a zero in North Woodstock, New Hampshire. And, yes, I had completed the trail. I sent a photo of me at Katahdin.

Later I was able to contact Harvest by e-mail and let her know about my completion. There were others I wanted to contact, but,

Chapter 10

What I Loved and What I Learned Hiking the Appalachian Trail

How I loved hiking the Appalachian Trial and the psychological and physical confidence that I developed in my ability to hike on — in good weather or bad. What a fabulous feeling it was to experience hard legs under me from hiking all those miles, as well as the strong arms, muscled up from the constant pushing of hiking poles. I was pleased that I was resourceful enough to figure out which "best habits" seemed to work for me.

It was as if I had the power to turn back the clock to when I was younger. That's one of the things I learned: Use it or lose it!

I learned that I'd better put up my tent before it got dark. I slept with a large-mouth peanut jar to accommodate the actions of my bladder and avoid having to get out of the tent at night. (I felt sorry for the women who could not use this method.) I also learned that the large-mouth jar must have a competent lid — or else!

I learned to keep my feet and hands covered with wool or synthetic gloves and socks at night. That is the best way to keep them from freezing, even tucked away inside a fifteen-degree sleeping bag. And I learned you have to take down your tent and food bag quickly on cold mornings; otherwise, your fingers freeze, especially if you have to take off your gloves like I did to accomplish the fine finger work that such activity required.

I learned how to keep my pack weight at twenty-five pounds, and even lower toward the end when I did the half-slack hiking through much of Pennsylvania and New Jersey. But I never hiked without a tent; that was a backup shelter for an emergency. Fortunately, I never needed it. The only time I ran out of food was when the bear stole it at Walnut Mountain in North Carolina, but even then Tommy and I were rescued by the cooler full of hiker goodies left by a Trail Angel at one of the road crossings.

As for injuries, I learned to bear up under constant numbness in the balls of my feet, just below the toes. But it was just part of hiking, and, for most hikers, numbness is temporary. In my case, I still have numbness, though improved.

From Tommy I learned how to apply mole skin with tape to reduce blistering of my toes. What a blessing!

Toward the end of the hike I stopped carrying a stove to prepare freeze-dried dinners. I carried GORP, candy bars and beef/chicken jerky — and that was great.

What I regretted most was not knowing anything about botany, about wildlife, about geology. Those who do know these areas of science "see" so much that I missed. It is like you only see what you know, and don't even know what you are missing if you don't know what to look for.

I made liberal use of motels along the way. That made it easier by my use of two vehicles, as well as the fact that I did have sufficient funds to do so. Still, I don't regret it. I'm not that much of a purist when it comes to such an adventure.

My advice to you, should you decide to hike the AT? Do the best you can and enjoy!

I do not recommend that most hikers use automobiles. There would probably not be enough parking places at the road-crossing trailheads if all hikers did. If you are young and healthy, you can do what most young thru-hikers do: push on up the trail until you run out of food and then somehow find a way to get into town for food and rest.

I was often astonished at the feats of young thru-hikers and their indomitable spirit. If you are in your sixties, you may be able to just push on like the young hikers — but maybe not. Consider using two vehicles until you get your hiking legs.

I enjoyed using two vehicles from the beginning and could not resist the temptation to continue the luxury when Tommy offered me his truck after he left the trail. I am in awe of those who seem to get by without frequently returning to the amenities of civilization.

Five days is the longest time I hiked without coming to one of my vehicles and civilization. I think frequent returns to civilization keep the spirits up and the negative feelings down.

One of the things I learned, as well, is how to cherish the memories, and I am reminded of that, most of all, when I'm with my brother Tommy. Recently I spent time with Tommy, and Tommy regaled a group of five relatives about our high adventure together, and he kept them in stitches. In fact, every time we get together we relive those days.

I recommend the trail to anyone who is in good health and who wants to try it. You don't have to be in top athletic condition to start, but the better your initial conditioning the easier the first month will be. After the first month, you are hardened with good hiking legs, and then it is only a matter of keeping a positive outlook. To keep the positive outlook, you have to love the hike in spite of all the hardship. You can't force yourself to love it. Why I loved it, I don't know, but I sure loved it.

If you don't love it, you will be constantly asking yourself, "Why am I still on the trail when I don't even have to be?" Or, to quote my brother, "Why get an ass-kicking every day when you don't deserve one?" You must protect yourself, and if you are truly miserable on the trail, it is better to take yourself off it, as Tommy did.

Finally, for those wanting to give the trail a try, I say, "Come on out and do it. It could be the best thing you have ever done!"

About the Author

Robert A. Callaway

Since completing my hike of the Appalachian Trail in 2008, I have continued to lead a busy life.

As for work, the old, civilian job in the pulmonary clinic at the Naval Hospital in Portsmouth, Virginia was closed, so I had to look around. I was able to find the same work in the pulmonary clinic at the Army Hospital in Fort Hood, Texas and worked there for eighteen months, until an Army pulmonary doctor returned from a deployment in Iraq. For the past year I have

Robert A. Callaway at Mount Moosilauke in New Hampshire.

worked in a pulmonary clinic in Green Bay, Wisconsin, two weeks per month. Two weeks on and two weeks off is just right. It keeps me on my toes, allows me to work in a field I love and then come home for life with Jane.

I have not done any hiking since coming off the trail. But I keep asking my brother Tommy and my other brother George to give it a go with me one day. So far, their answers are "Hell no!" and "Double hell no!" I have pushed the idea with my son, but he is not interested at this time. Several years ago he and I did 500 miles of biking in Florida and North Carolina, and he was a strong biker. Hopefully, I will get him to change his mind one day.

I have glaucoma. I had pre-glaucoma for fifteen years before I went on my hike and had been on eye drops for those fifteen years. I started noticing visual deficits while working in Texas. Going out on bike rides, I noted that when I looked into the safety mirror off the left side of my spectacles, I could not see as well as in the past. After returning to Virginia, I went to the ophthalmologist, who found significant visual loss in my left eye, and medications were intensified. I recently had surgery on the left eye, but it is now stable and the visual loss does not interfere with work, reading or driving.

As mentioned several times in the book, I am introverted and do not go out of my way to make friends. But during my trail experience, I found myself going out of my way to help other hikers, like driving them to the trail or to town and providing information about water sources and giving away trail maps. I had universally positive but usually brief interactions with fellow hikers, motel workers and grocery clerks. I never had an argument or altercation with anyone on or off the trail during my hike. So, despite Tommy's concerns about my introversion and about my hiking alone, I seemed to do okay. But I don't plan on throwing any parties anytime soon; I would be uncomfortable doing so. I took a Myers-Briggs Type Indicator® (MBTI®) personality inventory recently, and I do test as an introvert.

I do yoga and meditate regularly and find those practices more satisfying and fulfilling than the guilt-ridden approaches of the conservative Protestantism I grew up with as a child and young adult.

At age sixty-eight, I continue to run regularly. I enjoy reading novels, doing math problems, teaching math as a volunteer to students having trouble with it. I even read popular physics books by geniuses who try to make QED, gravity and relativity understandable to people like me. I probably don't really understand the physics concepts, because after closing such books I can't convey such information to others. But maybe it helps slow down mental aging, so I read as many as I can get my hands on.

So, for now, life is good.